W9-BOL-458

Holiday
Theme Parties

Entertaining Ideas, Decorations & Recipes
for Nine Unique Parties

Copyright © 2000
Creative Publishing international, Inc.
5900 Green Oak Drive
Minnetonka, Minnesota 55343
1-800-328-3895
All rights reserved
Printed in U.S.A.

President/CEO: David D. Murphy
Vice President/Editorial: Patricia K. Jacobsen
Vice President/Retail Sales & Marketing: Richard M. Miller

Holiday Theme Parties created by: The Editors of
  Creative Publishing international, Inc.

Executive Editor: Elaine Perry
Project Manager: Linnéa Christensen
Senior Editor: Linda Neubauer
Food Editor: Ellen Boeke
Senior Art Director: Stephanie Michaud
Cover Design: Mark Jacobson
Desktop Publishing Specialist: Laurie Kristensen
Project & Prop Stylists: Joanne Wawra and Christine Jahns
Food Prop Stylist: John Rajtar
Sample Production Staff: Arlene Dohrman, Sheila Duffy, Teresa Henn
Studio Services Manager: Marcia Chambers
Photo Services Coordinator: Carol Osterhus
Director of Photography: Chuck Nields
Photographers: Tate Carlson, Andrea Rugg
Technical Photo Stylists: Bridget Haugh, Christine Jahns
Food Stylists: Cathy Johnson, Cynthia Ojczyk, Bobbette Parker,
  Eugenie Zarling
Photography Services: Patrick Gibson
Shop Supervisor: Daniel Widerski
Director, Production Services: Kim Gerber
Contributors: C. M. Offray and Son, Inc.; Conso Products
  Company; Kunin Felt.

Printed on American paper by:
  R. R. Donnelley & Sons Co.
10 9 8 7 6 5 4 3 2 1

Creative Publishing international, Inc. offers a variety of how-to books. For
information write:
  Creative Publishing international, Inc.
    Subscriber Books
  5900 Green Oak Drive
  Minnetonka, MN 55343

Nutritional Information:
Each recipe includes nutrition information for the basic six nutrients as well as
exchanges for weight management. If a recipe has a range of servings, the data
applies to the greater number of servings. If alternate ingredients are listed, the
analysis applies to the first ingredient listed. Optional ingredients are not included
in the analysis.

Library of Congress Cataloging-in-Publication Data

Holiday theme parties : decorations, entertaining ideas & recipes for nine unique parties.
    p. cm.
  ISBN 0-86573-342-2
    1. Party decorations. 2. Holiday decorations. 3. Handicraft. 4. Holiday cookery. 5.
Entertaining. I. Creative Publishing International.

  TT900.P3 H64 2000
  745.594'1--dc21   00-029500

Holiday
Theme Parties

*Entertaining Ideas, Decorations & Recipes
for Nine Unique Parties*

CREATIVE
PUBLISHING
international

MINNETONKA, MINNESOTA

Contents

Trim the Tree 10

Tree trimming with appetizers and cocktails
followed by a hearty sit-down dinner.

Formal Evening 24

Intimate wine and cheese buffet plus select appetizers and desserts
to cap off a dressy evening affair.

Fun in the Snow 38

Multi-family outdoor winter fun
followed by a warm-you-up dinner buffet.

Caroling Dinner 50

Fabulous sit-down dinner to treat the "choir"
after an evening or afternoon songfest.

Open House Buffet 64

Self-service appetizer buffet welcoming neighbors
and friends to your home.

Introduction

Holiday entertaining is all about making memories; honoring the holidays with festive parties that will long be remembered for their originality, their great food, and their warm company. Organized planning, thorough preparation, and creative ideas are the keys to successfully hosting a marvelous party. Ultimately these three things

also ensure that you will be able to relax and enjoy the party right along with your guests.

Our goal in *Holiday Theme Parties* is to make the job of party hosting as effortless as possible. We have planned the invitations, favors, decorations, table settings, complete menus, and recipes for nine unique and memorable parties. Each party has its own signature style, whether it's our casual Cookie Exchange party or the Formal

Evening appetizer buffet. Some parties are planned for large groups, such as the holiday Open House Buffet, while others, like the Christmas Tea, are great for small circles of friends. We've included sit-down meals, buffet meals, and dessert and appetizer buffets, so no matter what your budget or seating situation, you can host a fabulous holiday party.

Beautifully photographed to help you see every detail, the parties are delightful and elegant. Yet they are designed to be effortless, with impressive ideas, delicious food, and handcrafted projects that are easy to do with minimal time. Materials lists and step-by-step instructions are provided when necessary, along with helpful tips and bright ideas that give you a hand in pulling off every party to perfection.

Parties

You're Invited

Trim the Tree

Formal Evening

Fun in the Snow

Caroling Dinner

Open House Buffet

Christmas Tea

Cookie Exchange

New Year's Eve Bash

Holiday Brunch

Trim the Tree

Holiday spirit comes alive when friends gather to decorate the Christmas tree. As each unique ornament nestles into its hand-picked spot, hearts recall stories of Christmases past and whisper hopes for bright tomorrows.

Menu

Spicy Party Shrimp

Pork Roast with Peppercorn Sauce

Squash Gratin

Steamed Green Beans

Wine-Poached Pear Salad

Caramel Ice Cream with
Iced Almonds

Introduce the tree-trimming theme by sending invitations that your guests transform into dimensional ornaments and bring with them to the party. With tree decorations as the focus, plan casual activities that encourage spontanaeity and conversation. If trimming your Christmas tree has always been a closely held family tradition, or if you prefer to decorate your tree in a specific style and color, consider setting up a "party tree" in another room or on a deck or patio, just for the event. Enjoy decorating the party tree with your friends without sacrificing your family traditions or preferences.

Highlight the evening with a festive dinner, seated around a table decorated to reflect the tree-trimming theme. Combine delicious food with spirited holiday festivities for a memorable holiday party.

Ornament Invitations

What You'll Need

- Stiff, reversible decorative papers
- Translucent vellum; letter-size (one sheet for every two invitations)
- Computer (optional)
- Metallic thread
- Envelopes, at least $4^{3}/8'' \times 5^{3}/4''$ (11.2 × 14.5 cm)

1. Cut a rectangle of decorative paper $8^{1}/2'' \times 5^{1}/2''$ (21.8 × 14 cm). Score the exact center with a butter knife; fold the paper in half along the scored line. Trace the ornament sections, one on each side of the fold, selecting a different design for each guest.

2. Print instructions and party information, two sets equally spaced, on letter–size vellum, using a computer. Or cut letter–size vellum in half and hand–print the information. Score the vellum and fold in half.

3. Insert the vellum inside the decorative paper. Tie the layers together along the fold, using metallic thread.

Our tree will be bare if you're not there!

Please join us for tree-trimming good company, and dinner.

When: Saturday, December 16, 7:00 p.m.

Where: The Neubauers

Please R.S.V.P., 555-1234, by December 9.

Turn this invitation into an ornament to hang on our tree. Here's how:

1. Cut out the two sections. Cut the slits exactly as marked.

2. Slide the sections together at right angles to each other.

3. Wrap the invitation card around opposite sides of the ornament and tie a knot at the very top. For the dove, string the cord through a tiny hole at the marked dot. Knot the cord ends together.

Feel free to get creative!

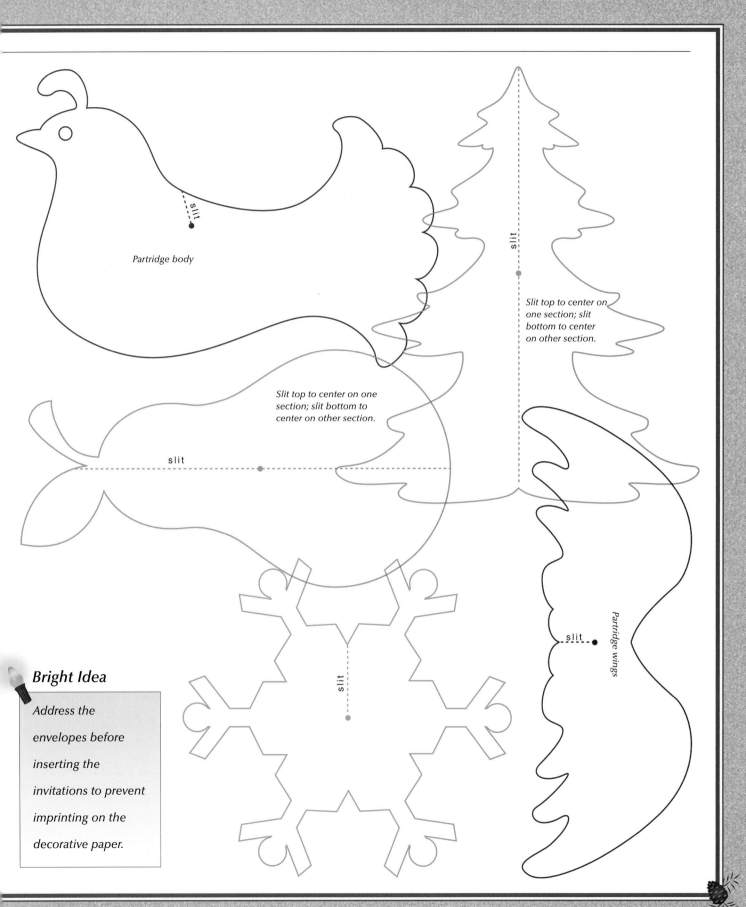

slit

Partridge body

slit

Slit top to center on
one section; slit
bottom to center
on other section.

Slit top to center on one
section; slit bottom to
center on other section.

slit

slit

Partridge wings

slit

Bright Idea

Address the
envelopes before
inserting the
invitations to prevent
imprinting on the
decorative paper.

Festive Garlands

Get the party rolling with a chatter-friendly garland-stringing session, accompanied by appetizers and cocktails. Set out bowls of garland ingredients, and thread long lengths of sturdy cording with a needle at each end, so your guests can work in pairs. String popcorn, pretzels, cranberries, and dried fruits, for an outdoor tree that treats winter birds. Or use colorful beads, metallic leaves, wrapped candies, tiny instruments, or bells for an indoor tree.

Bright Idea

Pop large kernel corn a day before the party, and store it in plastic bags in the refrigerator overnight. The popcorn will be less likely to shatter as you string it.

Tree Coasters

Cut simple tree shapes from green craft felt for quick and easy coasters. Add sequin ornaments and a star topper, if you feel ambitious.

Snack Servers

Offer your guests an appetizing snack mix, served in brightly painted tree-shaped cardboard boxes. Line each box with a cloth napkin.

Door Tree

Decorate a miniature half tree to hang on your front door, welcoming visitors into your home. If you are unable to find a half tree at your local craft or floral supply store, simply bend all of the branches on a full tree toward the front and sides. To avoid scratching the door, mount the tree on a felt banner.

What You'll Need

- Artificial half (or whole) pine tree with attached trunk, about 24" (61 cm) tall
- Five to eight floral picks in desired style and color
- 3 yd. (2.75 m) wired ribbon
- Floral wire; glue gun
- Felt rectangle, 72" × 22" (183 × 56 cm)
- Fusible web, 35" × 22" (89 × 56 cm)
- $3/8$" (1 cm) wooden dowel, 24" (61 cm) long
- Chair tie with tassels
- Dark green chenille stems

1. Fluff out branches of tree to a natural appearance. If you have purchased a full tree, bend all the branches toward the front and sides, so the tree rests flat on the table.

2. Arrange Christmas picks as desired. Secure them to the branches using hot glue or simply by twisting the branch wire around them.

3. Form a cluster bow (page 139) in the center of the ribbon, leaving long streamers. Wire the bow to the top of the tree, and arrange the streamers among the tree branches.

4. Fold felt in half. Fuse layers together, leaving unfused 1" (2.5 cm) from fold.

Fir Tree Favors

Pot fir tree seedlings, indigenous to your area, in clay pots tied with wired ribbon bows as parting favors for your guests. Arrange them in a miniature forest at the front door to give your entryway extra holiday flair.

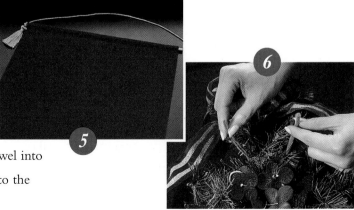

5. Cut the lower edge of the felt into a point. Stitch a 1" (2.5 cm) casing in the top of the felt. Insert the dowel into the casing. Tie the chair tie to the dowel ends for hanging.

6. Center the tree on the banner. Poke chenille stems through the banner from the back, and wrap them around the tree trunk to secure the tree to the banner.

String Trees Centerpiece

Create a light and airy display of string trees in various sizes to adorn the center of your table. Make the trees entirely of white string, or design them in a metallic theme. Arrange them in a landscape of fresh pine boughs studded with twinkling battery-operated lights.

1. Wrap the cone completely and smoothly with heavy plastic, forming a point at top; secure with tape. Apply a thin layer of liquid fabric stiffener to the outer surface of the cone, using a foam applicator.

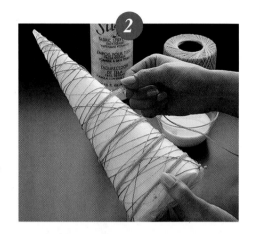

 ### *What You'll Need*

- Styrofoam® cones in various sizes
- Heavy plastic sheeting; tape
- Liquid fabric stiffener
- Foam applicator
- Wrapping materials, such as string, metallic cord, or narrow braid
- Glitter (optional)
- Newspaper
- Corkscrew
- Foil stars for tree toppers; hot glue or craft glue

2. Wrap string around cone, working from bottom to top at various angles. Secure string ends to cone, using pins. Add layers, covering surface to desired density.

3. Apply generous coat of liquid fabric stiffener over entire wrapped cone. Sprinkle with glitter, if desired.

4. Repeat steps 1 to 3 for as many trees as you want, in various sizes. Stand cones on newspaper to collect drips. Allow cones to dry completely.

5. Remove any pins. Insert corkscrew into bottom of cone. Slide dry string tree off cone, pulling on corkscrew. Remove any remaining residue between strings with nail file. Glue stars to tree tops.

Nature Print Napkins

Print a corner of each cloth napkin using a sprig of greenery, coated lightly on the back with fabric paint. For best results, use a flat variety, such as cedar. Apply the paint, using a foam applicator. Place the sprig on the napkin and press over it evenly with your fingers. Overlap two or three prints to create depth. Allow the prints to dry. Press them with a dry iron to heat-set the paint.

Tie each napkin with wired ribbon and insert a fresh green sprig as an accent.

Bright Idea

Coordinate the prints with your centerpiece. If you selected all white trees, print white greenery on the corners of dark green napkins. To accompany gold trees, print gold sprigs on white napkins.

Spicy Party Shrimp

Yield: 8 servings

Marinade:
- 2 tablespoons (25 mL) olive oil
- 2 tablespoons (25 mL) lime juice
- 2 tablespoons (25 mL) chili sauce or cocktail sauce
- 2 tablespoons (25 mL) finely chopped green onion
- 1 teaspoon (5 mL) minced garlic

- 1 teaspoon (5 mL) Dijon mustard
- 1 teaspoon (5 mL) hot pepper sauce (or more to taste)

- 1 lb. (450 g) large shrimp (35 to 40 count), cooked, peeled, and deveined (tails on)

Combine all marinade ingredients. Place in sealable plastic bag. Add shrimp. Seal bag and turn to coat shrimp. Refrigerate for at least 4 hours, turning shrimp occasionally to redistribute marinade.

Per Serving: Calories: 86 • Protein: 9 g. • Carbohydrate: 2 g. • Fat: 4 g.
• Cholesterol: 70 mg. • Sodium: 157 mg.
Exchanges: 1$^{1}/_{4}$ very lean meat, 1 fat

Pork Roast with Peppercorn Sauce

Yield: 8 to 10 servings

- 1 boneless pork top loin roast* (4 lbs./1.75 kg)
- 1 tablespoon (15 mL) olive oil
- 1 teaspoon (5 mL) salt
- $^{1}/_{2}$ teaspoon (2 mL) freshly ground pepper

Sauce:
- 1 tablespoon (15 mL) butter
- $^{1}/_{3}$ cup (75 mL) finely chopped shallots
- $^{1}/_{3}$ cup (75 mL) brandy
- 2 tablespoons (25 mL) green peppercorns in brine, drained
- 2 cups (500 mL) heavy cream
- $^{1}/_{2}$ teaspoon (2 mL) salt

Heat oven to 350°F/180°C. Rub roast with olive oil. Sprinkle evenly with salt and pepper all over. Place roast on rack in roasting pan. Roast for 50 minutes to 1 hour, or until internal temperature of roast is 145°F/63°C. Tent roast with foil. Let stand 10 minutes. (Internal temperature will go up at least 5°F/3°C while roast stands.)

While roast stands, make sauce. Melt butter in large skillet over medium heat. Add shallots and sauté for 3 to 4 minutes, or until tender. Add brandy. Reduce for 2 to 3 minutes, or until brandy is nearly gone. Add peppercorns and mash slightly with fork. Add cream. Simmer sauce for 4 to 5 minutes, or until reduced to a saucelike thickness, whisking occasionally. Stir in salt. Serve sauce with roast.

*A center-cut loin roast that is all one piece will cook more evenly and look nicer when sliced than a split and tied roast.

Per Serving: Calories: 509 • Protein: 37 g. • Carbohydrate: 2 g. • Fat: 38 g. • Cholesterol: 177 mg. • Sodium: 525 mg.
Exchanges: 5 lean meat, 4$^{3}/_{4}$ fat

Squash Gratin

Yield: 8 servings

- 2 medium yellow onions, chopped (3 cups/750 mL)
- 2 tablespoons (25 mL) olive oil
- 6 cups (1.5 L) shredded peeled butternut squash
- 2 tablespoons (25 mL) all-purpose flour
- 2 tablespoons (25 mL) butter, chopped
- 2 teaspoons (10 mL) salt
- 1/2 teaspoon (2 mL) freshly ground pepper
- 2 cups (500 mL) shredded Swiss cheese
- 1 cup (250 mL) whole milk or half-and-half

Topping:
- 3/4 cup (175 mL) dried bread crumbs
- 1/2 cup (125 mL) shredded Parmesan cheese
- 3 tablespoons (50 mL) butter, melted

Heat oven to 350°F/180°C. In a large skillet, cook onions in oil over medium heat for 20 to 25 minutes, or until onions are a deep golden brown (caramelized), stirring occasionally. While onions cook, butter-grease a 3-quart (3 L) casserole dish.

Spread 2 cups (500 mL) squash in prepared casserole. Top with half the onions, 1 tablespoon (15 mL) flour, 1 tablespoon (15 mL) butter, 1 teaspoon (5 mL) salt, and 1/4 teaspoon (1 mL) pepper. Sprinkle 1 cup (250 mL) cheese over top. Repeat. Top with remaining squash.

Pour milk over top. Combine topping ingredients. Sprinkle evenly over squash. Tent with foil. Bake for 50 to 60 minutes, or until top is golden brown and gratin is bubbly around edges, removing foil after 30 minutes.

Tip: Gratin can be assembled ahead and refrigerated until it is time to bake. If this is done, cool the onions before assembling gratin.

Per Serving: Calories: 359 • Protein: 14 g. • Carbohydrate: 29 g. • Fat: 22 g. • Cholesterol: 54 mg. • Sodium: 931 mg.
Exchanges: 1 1/4 high-fat meat, 1/2 starch, 4 vegetable, 2 fat

Wine-Poached Pear Salad

Yield: 8 servings

- 3 cups (750 mL) dry red wine (use a deep red like a Cabernet Sauvignon or Zinfandel)
- 1 cup (250 mL) orange juice
- $1/2$ cup (125 mL) sugar
- 2 tablespoons (25 mL) chopped crystallized ginger
- 1 stick cinnamon
- 4 Bosc pears, peeled, halved, and cored*
- 12 cups (3 L) mixed salad greens
- 1 cup (250 mL) vinaigrette salad dressing
- 1 cup (250 mL) walnut pieces, toasted**
- 1 cup (250 mL) crumbled blue cheese

Combine wine, orange juice, sugar, ginger, and cinnamon in large saucepan. Bring to a boil. Add pear halves, cut side down. Simmer for 20 minutes, turning pears over after 10 minutes. Remove pears from pan with slotted spoon. Cool slightly, then slice pears lengthwise, leaving them attached at the stem end. Fan pears out.

In a large mixing bowl, combine greens and vinaigrette. Toss to coat. Mound greens evenly on serving plates. Place one pear fan in center of each plate. Sprinkle salad evenly with walnuts and blue cheese.

To neatly core pears, use a melon baller to remove core from halved pears, then use a paring knife to carefully cut out stem.

**Toast walnuts in a skillet with 1 tablespoon (15 mL) butter. Sauté over medium heat until walnuts are toasted.*

Per Serving: Calories: 330 • Protein: 7 g. • Carbohydrate: 28 g. • Fat: 22 g. • Cholesterol: 11 mg. • Sodium: 661 mg.
Exchanges: $1/2$ high-fat meat, 1 vegetable, $11/2$ fruit, $31/2$ fat

Caramel Ice Cream

Yield: 4 cups (1 L)

- $1/3$ cup (75 mL) sugar
- $1/3$ cup (75 mL) heavy cream
- 3 cups (750 mL) half-and-half
- $1/2$ cup (125 mL) packed light brown sugar
- $1/4$ cup (60 mL) nonfat dry milk
- $1/4$ teaspoon (1 mL) salt
- 5 egg yolks
- 2 teaspoons (10 mL) vanilla extract

For caramel, place sugar in 2-quart (2 L) saucepan. Heat over medium-high heat until sugar melts, shaking pan occasionally. (Do not stir sugar or it will create lumps.) Cook melted sugar until a deep golden bown. (The darker it gets, the richer the flavor.) Remove from heat.

Gradually, whisk in cream. Be careful, because the mixture will bubble up quickly. Return to low heat. Cook and whisk for 1 minute. Set caramel aside and keep warm.

For ice cream base, combine half-and-half, brown sugar, nonfat dry milk, and salt in medium saucepan. Cook over medium heat until mixture reaches 165°F/74°C, stirring frequently. In a medium mixing bowl, whisk $1/2$ cup (125 mL) hot milk mixture into egg yolks. Return egg mixture to pan. Cook and stir over medium-low heat for 5 minutes. Whisk in warm caramel. Cook and stir for 5 minutes longer. Stir in vanilla.

Cover ice cream base with plastic wrap touching the surface. Cool at room temperature for 1 hour. Chill base in refrigerator for 4 hours or overnight. Freeze ice cream according to the manufacturer's directions for your ice cream maker. At this point, the ice cream will be like soft-serve ice cream. It can be eaten like this or placed in a plastic container and frozen until firm. Serve with Iced Almonds, right.

Note: This ice cream is quite rich, so a small amount is satisfying. For less rich ice cream, substitute 1 cup (250 mL) 2% or whole milk for 1 cup (250 mL) half-and-half.

Per $1/2$ Cup (125 mL): Calories: 282 • Protein: 5 g. • Carbohydrate: 27 g. • Fat: 17 g. • Cholesterol: 180 mg. • Sodium: 134 mg.
Exchanges: $1/4$ medium-fat meat, $1/2$ whole milk, $2 1/4$ fat, $1 1/2$ other carbohydrate

Iced Almonds

Yield: 4 cups (1 L)

- 2 cups (500 mL) whole blanched almonds
- 1 cup (250 mL) sugar
- $1/4$ cup (60 mL) butter
- 1 teaspoon (5 mL) vanilla extract
- $1/4$ teaspoon (1 mL) coarse salt

Combine almonds, sugar, and butter in large, heavy skillet. Cook over medium heat for 15 to 18 minutes after butter melts, until almonds are toasted and sugar is brown and syrupy, stirring occasionally. Remove from heat. Stir in vanilla.

Spread mixture on ungreased sheet of foil. Sprinkle evenly with salt. Cool. When almonds are cool and set, break them into 3- to 4-almond chunks. Store in airtight container. Serve with Caramel Ice Cream, left.

Per $1/4$ Cup (60 mL): Calories: 181 • Protein: 4 g. • Carbohydrate: 16 g. • Fat: 12 g. • Cholesterol: 8 mg. • Sodium: 54 mg.
Exchanges: $1/2$ high-fat meat, $1 1/2$ fat, 1 other carbohydrate

Formal Evening

After a night at the opera, theater, or a holiday concert, friends gather to applaud the event and toast the season. Dressed to the nines, the guests are the center of attraction at this brief, yet sophisticated affair.

Menu

Wine and Cheese Buffet

Salmon Crescents

Melon and Prosciutto Platter

Crepe Cones

Chocolate Espresso Torte

Tangy Lemon Tartlets

Simplify your plans and still throw an impressive party, giving your attention to carefully appointed accents, a small buffet of superb wines and cheeses, and a few choice appetizers and desserts. In keeping with the formal tone of the evening, use your finest glassware and serving pieces, displayed in luxurious fashion. Follow a crisp black and white scheme, with gold metallic accents, a perfect complement to the formal attire of your guests. Add the warm glow of candlelight with delicate, fragrant flowers for a truly elegant atmosphere.

Whether the party is held before or after the evening's entertainment, time will be limited. Set up as much as possible beforehand, allowing plenty of time to relax and get dressed up yourself. Then, upon arriving home after the event or just before the first guests arrive, set out the food on the buffet table, open the wine, and light the candles. Let the magic begin!

Grape Invitations

What You'll Need

- Elegant white single-fold blank cards
- Computer (optional)
- Black paper
- Scissors with deckle blades
- Metallic gold craft paint
- Small sponge pouncer, available at craft stores
- Paper punch
- Gold silk leaves
- Narrow gold sheer ribbon
- Envelopes

1. Print your party message on the inside of the card, orienting the copy vertically. Cut black paper 1" (2.5 cm) narrower and shorter than the card front, using scissors with deckle blades.

2. Pour a small amount of gold paint onto a paper plate. Dip a sponge pouncer into the paint; remove excess. Pounce circles on the black paper, overlapping and layering them to form a grape cluster. Reload paint as neccessary. Allow to dry.

3. Center the black paper over the card front. Punch two small holes at the top of the grape cluster, through the black paper and the card front. Cut a small slit in each gold silk leaf. Tie all together with narrow sheer ribbon.

Grapevine Wreath

Echo the theme of the invitations with a lit grape-vine wreath, welcoming your late-night guests to your home.

What You'll Need

- Grapevine wreath, 18" (46 cm)
- White battery-operated lights
- Floral wire
- Gold decorative cord with tassels
- Several clusters of gilded grapes with leaves

1. Wrap the lights evenly throughout the wreath. Secure the battery pack for the lights to the back of the wreath, at the top center, using floral wire.

2. Wind decorative cord around the wreath, beginning and ending at the top. Allow the tasseled ends to drape into the wreath center.

3. Wire three or four clusters of grapes to the top of the wreath, on each side of the center.

Bright Idea

Spray-paint the wreath white before embellishing it, if you plan to hang it on a dark surface.

27

Appetizer and Dessert Buffet

Drape the table with gold metallic fabric. Add wide black satin ribbon streamers as an accent under each serving piece. Identify each wonderful appetizer and dessert with elegantly printed cards.

Floating Candles

For a stunning coffee table accent, weave a square mat from an assortment of black and gold ribbons. Place a shallow clear glass bowl atop the mat; cover the bottom of the bowl with clear glass marbles. Fill the bowl with water and float gold candles and large white flower heads.

Fireplace Glow

What You'll Need
- Black foam-core board
- Wide clear tape
- Metallic gold foil
- Double-stick tape
- Gold thumbtacks (optional)
- 12" (30.5 cm) mirror tile

Late night may not be the best time to start a cozy fire, especially dressed in a tuxedo. But you can still create a lovely glow with a grouping of candles.

1. Cut a rectangle of foam-core to fit the fireplace grate, for the candle platform. Cut a second rectangle the same width and about 20" (51 cm) high, for the reflective back.

2. Prop the back upright behind the platform. Hinge the pieces together with wide clear tape, taping from both the front and back.

3. Cut a 4" (10 cm) square of foam-core in half diagonally. Tape the triangles to the platform and back to support the hinge.

4. Cut a piece of gold foil paper the height of the back and 5" (12 cm) wider than the back. Fanfold the paper. Unfold and secure it to the back, using double-stick tape along the edges. Add gold thumbtacks, if desired.

5. Place the foam-core platform on the fireplace grate. Place the mirror tile on the platform and arrange the pillar candles on the tile.

Wine Bottle Coasters

Make gilded wine bottle coasters from humble 4" (10 cm) clay pot saucers. Simply spray paint them! Apply protective felt pads to the bottom.

Beaded Napkins

Add an unexpected touch of class to plain cocktail napkins by hand-sewing a tiny gold bead or jingle bell at each corner. Pick up each napkin from the center and insert it into a wine glass, fanning out the corners.

Wine Bottle Favors

What You'll Need

- Single-serving wine bottles
- Nine gold jingle bells in assorted sizes, for each favor
- 24-gauge brass wire, about 8" (20.5 cm) for each favor
- Wire cutter
- Ribbon

1. Cut an 8" (20.5 cm) piece of brass wire. Secure a small jingle bell to one end of the wire, twisting the wire end around itself. Insert the other end of the wire through the remaining jingle bells, staggering the bells from side to side and increasing in size, to resemble a grape cluster.

2. At the top of the bell cluster, form a loop in the wire to keep the bells in place; twist the wire to secure. Trim off any excess wire.

3. Insert ribbon through the wire loop, wrap it around the bottle neck, and tie a bow above the bells. After removing the bell cluster from the bottle, it can be used as a tree ornament.

Wine and Cheese Buffet

Nothing could be simpler or more elegant than a wine and cheese buffet. All it takes are a few well-chosen cheeses and suitable wines. Many good wine stores have cheese counters and a knowledgeable staff to help you, so you can get everything in one stop. Larger supermarkets also carry an excellent selection of cheeses in their deli departments.

Cheeses: Figure that you'll need 4 to 6 ounces (125 to 170 g) of cheese per guest. Buy whole cheeses or large pieces for best quality. A balanced variety is the key when selecting cheeses for your party—variety in types and texture (soft, hard, semisoft, blue), levels of flavor (strong, mild, sharp), and milk types (cow, sheep, goat). Don't overdo it, though. It's less overwhelming to your guests, and more affordable for you, if you buy just four or five nice cheeses to sample.

When presenting your cheese assortment, place cheeses on individual cutting boards or large cutting boards, leaving plenty of space between each cheese. Place whole pieces out with knives so guests can cut off slices for themselves. If you slice the cheese first, it will only dry out. Make sure to label each cheese, too, and possibly include a brief description of its flavor.

Wine: Choosing wine to go with cheese isn't as hard as you might think. If you are serving several cheeses, serve several wines. There are some classic pairings, of course, like Port wine with Stilton blue cheese. Or you might select

wines from the same region of the world as the cheese, like Spanish Rioja with Cabrales cheese. What's most important is that the selection of wines and cheeses don't overwhelm each other. Again, balance is key. A great cheese will make an average wine better, but an average cheese will drag down a great wine. If you have to choose, put your money into getting really good cheese.

Accompaniments: Along with your cheese boards and bottles of wine, there are a few other goodies that will make your party table complete. Offer baskets of crusty French bread or plain, flatbread-type crackers. Fruit is another tasty and attractive accompaniment. Fresh apples, pears, plums, and grapes are the obvious choices, but dried fruit, like dates, figs, and prunes are excellent with cheese. Cured olives, such as kalamatas or Nicoise, are also wonderful with wine and cheese. Marinated mixed olives are often available in cheese stores or in the deli department of supermarkets. Finally, toasted nuts, like almonds, walnuts, or hazelnuts, are ideal with cheese.

Yield: 48 crescents

- 4 oz. (125 g) smoked salmon, flaked
- $1/4$ cup (60 mL) sour cream or mayonnaise
- $1/2$ teaspoon (2 mL) lemon juice
- $1/4$ teaspoon (1 mL) dried dillweed, or 1 teaspoon (5 mL) snipped fresh dillweed
- $1/4$ teaspoon (1 mL) salt (optional)
- $1/4$ teaspoon (1 mL) freshly ground pepper
- 1 egg
- 1 tablespoon (15 mL) water
- 1 pkg. (17 oz./500 g) frozen puff pastry dough, thawed

Salmon Crescents

In a small bowl, combine salmon, sour cream, lemon juice, dillweed, salt, and pepper. Set filling aside.

Beat egg and water together in small bowl. Roll one sheet of puff pastry into a 16" × 12" (40.5 × 30.5 cm) rectangle. Cut 24 rounds out of dough using a 2½" (6.5 cm) round cutter. Spoon 1 teaspoon (5 mL) filling in center of each round. Brush edges of rounds with egg mixture. Fold dough over filling so edges match, pressing with tines of fork to seal. Place crescents on large baking sheet. Repeat with remaining dough and filling.

Brush tops of all crescents with egg mixture. Pierce tops of crescents once with knife tip. (Crescents may be covered with plastic wrap and refrigerated for several hours at this point.) Heat oven to 400°F/200°C. Bake for 12 to 15 minutes, or until crescents are golden brown.

Per 2 Crescents: Calories: 124 • Protein: 3 g. • Carbohydrate: 9 g. • Fat: 9 g. • Cholesterol: 11 mg. • Sodium: 148 mg.
Exchanges: $1/8$ lean meat, $2/3$ starch, $1^1/2$ fat

Melon and Prosciutto Platter

Melons and prosciutto ham make a classic Italian pairing that is both simple and elegant. Arrange slices of cantaloupe and honeydew melon on a platter with ribbons of prosciutto folded between them for a beautiful presentation that needs no garnish. Or, skewer chunks of melon on long party picks with rolled or accordion-folded pieces of prosciutto. A high-quality deli-sliced ham can be substituted for prosciutto, but it's worth the effort if you can find the real thing.

Crepe Cones

Yield: 32 cones

Crepes:
- $3/4$ cup (175 mL) all-purpose flour
- $1/4$ to $1/2$ teaspoon (1 to 2 mL) cracked black pepper
- Pinch salt
- 1 cup (250 mL) milk
- 1 whole egg
- 1 egg yolk
- 2 tablespoons (25 mL) butter, melted

- 2 pkgs. (5 oz./150 g each) soft herbed cheese (like Boursin or Rondelé)
- 2 cups (500 mL) julienned bell peppers (any color), carrots, jicama, or blanched asparagus ($2''$ x $1/8''$/5 cm x 3 mm strips)
- Fresh chives

For crepes, place flour, pepper, and salt in medium mixing bowl. In second bowl, whisk milk, egg, yolk, and butter together. Gradually whisk milk mixture into flour. Cover. Chill for 30 minutes.

Heat $10''$ (25.5 cm) skillet over medium–high heat. Wipe pan with paper towel dipped in vegetable oil. Whisk batter again. Add about 3 tablespoons (50 mL) batter to hot skillet, swirling pan quickly to spread batter over bottom of pan. (If batter is too thick and doesn't spread quickly, whisk 1 or 2 tablespoons/15 or 25 mL more milk into batter.) Cook crepe for about 30 seconds, or until browned on the bottom. Turn crepe over and cook for another 30 seconds. Transfer crepe to plate. Repeat with remaining batter, wiping pan with oil before making each crepe. You should get 8 crepes.

For cones, spread about 2 tablespoons (25 mL) cheese on each crepe to within $1/2''$ (1.3 cm) of edge. Cut each crepe into quarters. Arrange some vegetable strips and a couple of chives on quarters closer to the edges than the points. (You want the vegetables to stick out of the tops of the cones.) Roll quarters into cones. Roll back edges of cones to reveal more vegetables. Cover with plastic wrap and refrigerate cones for a few hours before serving.

Tip: Crepes can be made a day ahead and kept refrigerated covered with plastic wrap.

Per 2 Cones: Calories: 127 • Protein: 3 g. • Carbohydrate: 6 g. • Fat: 10 g. • Cholesterol: 53 mg. • Sodium: 144 mg. Exchanges: $1/4$ high-fat meat, $1/4$ starch, $1/4$ vegetable, $1 3/4$ fat

Chocolate Espresso Torte

Yield: 16 servings

Torte:
- 12 oz. (340 g) semisweet chocolate, chopped
- 1 lb. (500 g) butter
- 1 cup (250 mL) freshly brewed espresso
- 1 cup (250 mL) packed brown sugar
- 8 eggs, slightly beaten

Ganache:
- 8 oz. (227 g) semisweet chocolate, chopped
- $2/3$ cup (150 mL) heavy cream
- 2 tablespoons (25 mL) butter, cut up

- 16 dried apricots
- 16 fresh strawberries

Heat oven to 350°F/180°C. Line a 9" (23 cm) springform pan* with parchment paper. Begin heating water for water bath.

For torte, place 12 ounces (340 g) chocolate in medium mixing bowl. In medium saucepan, bring 1 pound (500 g) butter, the espresso, and sugar to a boil over medium-high heat, stirring until sugar is dissolved. Pour hot espresso mixture over chocolate. Whisk until chocolate is melted and smooth. Gradually whisk in beaten eggs.

Pour batter into prepared pan. Place springform pan in large roasting pan. Set pan in oven, then fill with hot water until it comes $1/3$ to $1/2$ up sides of springform pan. Bake for 1 hour to 1 hour 10 minutes, or until nearly set in the middle. Remove springform pan from water and place on cooling rack. Run a sharp knife around the edge of the torte, but don't loosen sides of pan. Cool completely, then refrigerate torte for several hours or overnight.

For ganache, place 8 ounces (227 g) chocolate in medium mixing bowl. In small saucepan, heat cream and butter over medium heat until butter melts and mixture starts to boil. Pour hot mixture over chocolate. Whisk until chocolate is melted and smooth. Let cool to room temperature. (If desired, dip apricots or strawberries halfway into ganache. Set aside on wax-paper-lined plate.)

Remove sides from torte pan. Invert serving plate on top of torte, then turn everything over. Remove bottom of pan and parchment paper. Smooth sides and top of torte with metal spatula. Spread thin layer of ganache over top and sides of torte. As ganache sets on cold torte, spread one or two more layers of ganache over top. (The thickness of the ganache is up to you. You can continue to spread layers of ganache over torte until all the ganache is used up, or save any extra ganache and use it as an ice cream topping.)

Garnish torte with apricots and strawberries, placing them on outside edge of torte. Chill torte until 1 hour before serving time. (Like cheese, this torte tastes best when it has a chance to warm up slightly.)

The batter for this cake is fairly thin. You need a good, tight-fitting springform pan or the batter may leak out.

Per Serving: Calories: 527 • Protein: 5 g. • Carbohydrate: 41 g. • Fat: 41 g.
• Cholesterol: 186 mg. • Sodium: 295 mg.
Exchanges: $1/2$ medium-fat meat, $1/2$ starch, $1/4$ fruit, 7 fat, 2 other carbohydrate

Tangy Lemon Tartlets

Yield: 30 tartlets

Pastry:
- 1 cup (250 mL) all-purpose flour
- 1/2 cup (125 mL) powdered sugar
- 1/4 cup (60 mL) butter, chilled and diced
- Pinch salt
- 2 to 3 tablespoons (25 to 50 mL) ice water

Filling:
- 1/2 cup (125 mL) fresh lemon juice
- 7 tablespoons (110 mL) butter
- 1/4 cup (60 mL) water
- 1 1/2 teaspoons (7 mL) grated lemon peel
- 3/4 cup (175 mL) granulated sugar
- 3 tablespoons (50 mL) cornstarch
- Pinch salt
- 3 egg yolks
- 1 whole egg
- 1 1/2 teaspoons (7 mL) almond-flavored liqueur (optional)
- Whipped cream

For pastry, combine flour, powdered sugar, butter, and salt in food processor. Process until mixture resembles coarse cornmeal. With motor running, drizzle in water, 1 tablespoon (15 mL) at a time, until dough clings and forms a ball. Wrap dough in plastic wrap, flatten into a disk, and chill for at least 30 minutes.

Heat oven to 400°F/200°C. Roll dough to 1/8" (3 mm) thickness. Cut out 30 rounds of dough using a 2 1/2" (6.5 cm) round cutter, rerolling dough scraps if necessary. Place dough circles in cups of mini-muffin tins. Prick bottom of tart crusts with fork. Bake for 8 to 10 minutes, or until golden brown. Cool crusts on wire racks. (Crusts may be made several days in advance and stored in an airtight container.)

For filling, combine lemon juice, butter, water, and lemon peel in medium saucepan. Heat over medium heat until butter melts. Remove from heat. In medium mixing bowl, whisk together granulated sugar, cornstarch, and salt. Whisk in yolks and egg. Gradually whisk in hot juice mixture. Return mixture to pan. Cook over medium heat for 5 to 7 minutes, or until filling is thick and bubbly, whisking constantly. Remove from heat. Whisk in liqueur, if desired.

Spoon 1 tablespoon (15 mL) filling into each tart crust. Cover with plastic wrap and chill for several hours before serving. Garnish each serving with dab of whipped cream.

Notes: Instead of making fresh tart crusts, purchase frozen phyllo dough shells or pre-made tart/hors d'oeuvre shells.

Tartlets can be made up to a day ahead. Garnish with whipped cream just before serving.

Per Tartlet: Calories: 92 • Protein: 1 g. • Carbohydrate: 11 g. • Fat: 5 g.
• Cholesterol: 40 mg. • Sodium: 55 mg.
Exchanges: 1/4 starch, 1 fat, 1/2 other carbohydrate

Fun in the Snow

Nature sets the stage for this fun-filled family party, with a billowy blanket of fluffy white snow. There's nothing like an exhilarating toboggan ride to urge gleeful giggles from children and help grownups shed their weekday worries.

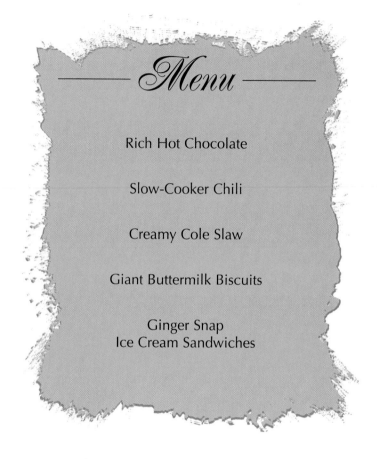

— Menu —

Rich Hot Chocolate

Slow-Cooker Chili

Creamy Cole Slaw

Giant Buttermilk Biscuits

Ginger Snap
Ice Cream Sandwiches

Outdoor winter fun could also include ice skating, skiing, or snow boarding. And when the snow is right for packing, there are snowmen to be made, snow forts to be built, and snowballs to be thrown. Your guests will arrive at your door afterward with cold hands and hearty appetites. Greet them with the tantalizing aromas of home-baked biscuits and spicy chili wafting from the kitchen and offer hand-warming mugs of hot chocolate.

Delight the children as well as the adults with decorations and table accents that have a casual style and an obvious sense of humor. With a totally made-ahead buffet dinner and a laid-back attitude, enjoy the party as if you were a kid again.

One mitten reads: "Please join the Michaud family for an afternoon of fun in the SNOW!"

Mitten Invitations

Purchase thin wooden mitten shapes from a craft supply store; one pair for each family on the invitation list. Or cut mitten shapes from thin balsa wood. Paint the mittens with a base coat of acrylic craft paint. Add simple designs to the fronts, and write party information on the backs using paint pens. Join the mittens with a strip of leather lacing. Your guests can keep the invitation as a memento and hang it on their family Christmas tree.

Bright Idea

Prepare an entrance area with washable rugs and lots of hangers for removing and drying outerwear and boots. Set a broom just outside the door for brushing off snow-encrusted kids. Your guests will appreciate the convenience and you will keep the outdoors outdoors.

Welcome Sled

Decorate a rustic sled with a spray of fresh greenery and berries tied up with a colorful bow. Prop the sled against the house near the front entry.

What You'll Need
- Floral foam block
- Paddle floral wire; wire cutter
- Several evergreen branches
- Fresh or artificial winter berries on stems
- Wired ribbon

1. Secure the floral foam to the sled using paddle floral wire.

2. Cut evergreen branches in graduated lengths. Insert longer branches, pointing downward, into the bottom of the floral foam. Add gradually shorter branches, working in toward the top and covering the foam completely. Insert top branches pointing upward.

3. Insert berry stems.

4. Make a cluster bow (page 139) from the wired ribbon, leaving long tails. Wire the bow near the top of the arrangement.

41

Mitten-Drying Garland

Invite your guests to hang their wet mittens and hats from the prepared fireplace garland. Simply attach clothespins with floral wire, hidden in the greenery. Make sure you secure the garland in a way that can support the added weight.

What You'll Need

- Artificial garland (fresh garland is dangerous near the fireplace)
- Spring-style clothespins
- Paddle floral wire
- 1×2 board cut to the length of the mantel
- Paint or stain to match the mantel
- Two clamps
- Eye screws

1. Paint or stain the 1×2 mounting board to match the mantel. Allow it to dry. Secure the board to the mantel, using small clamps.

2. Attach eye screws to mounting board at ends and at evenly spaced intervals for draping the garland. Secure the garland to the eye screws using floral wire.

3. Secure the clothespins to the garland at regular intervals, using floral wire.

4. Make traditional ribbon bows (page 138). Attach a bow at each end of the mounting board.

Snow-Covered Tabletop

Felt cut to size makes a quick and easy tablecloth. Snowflakes cut from white flannel cling to the felt, serving as placemats.

Melted Snowman Centerpiece

Indoors where it's toasty warm a snowman's minutes are numbered. Accessories left behind by a melted snowman make a cute conversation-starting centerpiece.

Snowball Place Cards

"I've got a snowball here with your name on it!" No need to duck; it's merely marking your special place at the table.

What You'll Need

- Styrofoam® balls, 3" (7.5 cm) in diameter; one for each guest
- Artificial snow paste, such as Snow Accents
- Palette knife
- Mat knife
- Card stock or precut place cards
- Snowflake stamp; stamp pad

1. Cut a slice from the Styrofoam ball to flatten the bottom.

2. Apply a thin coat of snow paste to the ball, using a palette knife. For ease in handling, poke a chop stick or pencil up into the ball through the bottom. Allow the snowball to dry thoroughly.

3. Make a shallow slit into the top of the snowball for inserting the place card. Stamp snowflakes on the place card and write the guest's name. Insert the place card into the slit.

Scarf Napkin Rings

Roll each flatware setting in a napkin tied with a tiny scarf. Cut fleece strips 2" × 22" (5 × 56 cm). Fringe the ends by cutting 1½" (3.8 cm) slits, ¼" (6 mm) apart.

Wintry Buffet

With white quilt batting thrown over sturdy boxes, create snowy hills for your buffet table. Purchase wooden sleds from the craft store, and use them as handy trays to hold condiments.

Bright Idea

Avoid candles when children are among the guests. Instead, create a festive mood with strings of twinkling Christmas lights.

Slow-Cooker Chili

Yield: 12 cups (3 L)

- 1 lb. (450 g) ground turkey or beef
- 1 lb. (450 g) ground Italian sausage (mild or spicy)
- 1 tablespoon (15 mL) vegetable oil
- 1 medium onion, chopped (1½ cups/375 mL)
- 2 teaspoons (10 mL) minced garlic
- 2 cans (15 oz./450 g each) black beans, rinsed and drained
- 1 can (28 oz./790 g) diced tomatoes, undrained

- 1 bottle (12 oz./340 g) chili sauce
- 2 cans (4.5 oz./130 g each) diced green chiles
- ½ cup (125 mL) water
- 1 tablespoon (15 mL) chili powder
- 2 teaspoons (10 mL) unsweetened cocoa
- 2 teaspoons (10 mL) dried oregano leaves
- 1 teaspoon (5 mL) ground cumin
- ¼ to ½ teaspoon (1 to 2 mL) cayenne pepper (optional)

Brown turkey and sausage in large skillet over medium heat. Transfer meat to 3½-quart (3.5 L) slow cooker with a slotted spoon. Wipe out skillet. Add oil to skillet and heat over medium heat. Add onion and garlic. Sauté for 6 to 8 minutes, or until onion is tender. Add onion and garlic to slow cooker. Add remaining ingredients to slow cooker and mix well.

Cover slow cooker and cook on high until chili starts to simmer. Reduce heat to low. Cook at least 2 hours, stirring occasionally.

Serve chili with shredded cheese, sour cream, and sliced green onions for optional garnishes.

Per 1 Cup (250 mL): Calories: 262 • Protein: 17 g. • Carbohydrate: 21 g. • Fat: 13 g. • Cholesterol: 41 mg. • Sodium: 1,016 mg.
Exchanges: 1½ lean meat, ½ starch, 2½ vegetable, 1½ fat

Creamy Cole Slaw

Yield: 8 cups (2 L)

- 1 pkg. (16 oz./450 g) classic cole slaw mix
- 1 pkg. (16 oz./450 g) broccoli cole slaw mix
- 2½ cups (625 mL) shredded tart red apples, unpeeled, cored
- 1 cup (250 mL) shredded carrots

Dressing:
- 1½ cups (375 mL) mayonnaise
- ¾ cup (175 mL) sour cream
- 2 tablespoons (25 mL) sugar
- 2 tablespoons (25 mL) apple cider vinegar
- 1 teaspoon (5 mL) celery salt
- ½ teaspoon (2 mL) freshly ground pepper
- ¼ teaspoon (1 mL) salt

In a large bowl, combine cole slaw mixes, apples, and carrots. Mix well. In second bowl, whisk together dressing ingredients. Add dressing to slaw. Mix well to coat. Cover. Chill at least 2 hours, stirring once or twice.

Per ½ Cup (125 mL) : Calories: 210 • Protein: 2 g. • Carbohydrate: 9 g. • Fat: 19 g. • Cholesterol: 17 mg. • Sodium: 213 mg.
Exchanges: 1½ vegetable, ⅛ fruit, 3¾ fat

Giant Buttermilk Biscuits

Yield: 12 biscuits

- $2^{1}/_{2}$ cups (625 mL) all-purpose flour, divided
- $1^{1}/_{2}$ cups (375 mL) cake flour
- 2 tablespoons (25 mL) sugar
- 1 tablespoon (15 mL) baking powder
- $1^{1}/_{2}$ teaspoons (7 mL) salt
- $1/_{4}$ teaspoon (1 mL) baking soda
- $1/_{3}$ cup (75 mL) vegetable shortening, chilled and cubed
- $2^{1}/_{4}$ cups (550 mL) fresh buttermilk
- 2 tablespoons (25 mL) butter, melted

Heat oven to 475°F/240°C. Spray two 8" (20.5 cm) round pans with nonstick vegetable cooking spray. In large bowl, combine 2 cups (500 mL) all-purpose flour, the cake flour, sugar, baking powder, salt, and baking soda. Cut shortening into flour mixture until pea-sized. Stir in buttermilk until flour is completely moistened. (Dough will be wet.)

Sprinkle a heavy layer of remaining all-purpose flour on work surface. Turn dough onto flour and sprinkle a heavy layer of flour on top. Gently pat and shape dough into rectangle, 1" (2.5 cm) thick.

Use a floured $2^{1}/_{2}$" (6.5 cm) round cutter to cut dough into biscuits. Transfer biscuits to pans, 6 biscuits per pan. (Use a spatula for easy transfer.) Gently reroll scraps, being careful not to overwork the dough. Brush tops of biscuits with melted butter. Bake for 15 to 17 minutes, or until biscuits are golden brown on top. Serve immediately, or cool on a wire rack and reheat before serving.

Note: The secret to fluffy biscuits is the wet dough. The moisture produces lots of steam to raise these biscuits high.

Per Biscuit: Calories: 239 • Protein: 5 g. • Carbohydrate: 35 g. • Fat: 8 g. • Cholesterol: 7 mg. • Sodium: 507 mg. Exchanges: $2^{1}/_{4}$ starch, $1^{1}/_{2}$ fat

Bright Idea

Allow 45 minutes to an hour for guests to arrive, have a drink, and mingle before calling them into the dining room for dinner.

Ginger Snap Ice Cream Sandwiches

Yield: 24 sandwiches

- $1/2$ cup (125 mL) sugar
- $1/2$ cup (125 mL) butter
- $1/4$ cup (59 mL) dark molasses
- 1 tablespoon (15 mL) brandy
- $2^1/4$ cups (550 mL) all-purpose flour, divided
- 1 teaspoon (5 mL) ground ginger
- 1 teaspoon (5 mL) ground allspice
- $1/4$ teaspoon (1 mL) salt
- $4^1/2$ cups (1.125 L) ice cream (vanilla, caramel pecan, cinnamon), slightly softened

Heat oven to 350°F/180°C. In 1-quart (1 L) saucepan, combine sugar, butter, and molasses. Bring to a boil over medium heat, stirring constantly. Remove from heat. Stir in brandy. (Mixture will bubble up slightly.) Set aside.

In large mixing bowl, combine 1 cup (250 mL) flour, the ginger, allspice, and salt. Add molasses mixture. Beat at medium speed of electric mixer until well blended. Stir in enough of remaining flour to make a stiff dough.

Roll out one-fourth of the dough to $1/8$" to $1/4$" (3 to 6 mm) thickness. Cut into $2^1/2$" (6.5 cm) rounds. Transfer to ungreased baking sheet. Reroll scraps. (Do not reroll more than once. It will overwork the dough, making very tough cookies.) Bake cookies for 6 to 8 minutes, or until set. Immediately remove from baking sheet to wire rack. Continue rolling and baking remaining dough.

After cookies have completely cooled, spoon and smooth about 3 tablespoons (50 mL) ice cream onto half of the cookies. Top with remaining cookies to make sandwiches. Wrap individual sandwiches in plastic wrap and freeze.

Tip: For more festive cookies, use a cookie cutter with a scalloped edge or some other design. Then cut a block of ice cream into $3/4$" (2 cm) slices. Use the same cookie cutter to cut out matching pieces of ice cream.

Per Sandwich: Calories: 151 • Protein: 2 g. • Carbohydrate: 21 g. • Fat: 7 g. • Cholesterol: 21 mg. • Sodium: 85 mg. Exchanges: $1/2$ starch, $1^1/4$ fat, 1 other carbohydrate

Rich Hot Chocolate

Yield: 9 cups (2.25 L)

- 1 cup (250 mL) sugar
- $1/2$ cup (125 mL) unsweetened Dutch-process cocoa
- $1/4$ teaspoon (1 mL) salt
- 5 cups (1.25 L) water
- 2 cups (500 mL) 1% milk
- 1 cup (250 mL) heavy cream

In a 3-quart (3 L) saucepan, combine sugar, cocoa, and salt. Whisk in water. Bring to a boil over high heat, stirring until sugar is dissolved. Reduce heat to medium. Add milk and cream. Heat through. Keep warm over low heat. Serve chocolate topped with marshmallows or whipped cream sprinkled with crushed peppermint candy.

Per 1 Cup: Calories: 212 • Protein: 3 g. • Carbohydrate: 28 g. • Fat: 11 g. • Cholesterol: 38 mg. • Sodium: 135 mg.
Exchanges: $1/4$ low-fat milk, 2 fat, $1 1/2$ other carbohydrate

Caroling Dinner

Voices joined in harmony, whether perfect in pitch or slightly off-key, set a joyful tone for your holiday party. With familiar carols and spirited jingle-bell tunes, friends and family revel in the chance to sing for this fabulous supper.

Menu

Wassail

White Bean-
Sundried Tomato Crostini

Spicy Italian Breadsticks

Italian-Style Lasagna

Roasted Asparagus

Chocolate Swirl Cheesecake

Plan a night of caroling and camaraderie. Whether you sing at a local nursing home, troop through your neighborhood, or hold a rousing songfest around your own piano, everyone will enjoy the fellowship and music. If you sense a bit of reluctance among your guests, or perhaps lack a confident accompanist, try caroling karaoke-style, with a microphone connected to your sound system. Be sure to inform your guests if you intend to spend part of the evening out in cold weather, so they come appropriately dressed.

Follow the caroling theme from the invitations to the holiday decor throughout your home, using tiny musical instruments, bells, and music symbols. End the evening on a high note with a festive sit-down dinner around a table decorated with an unmistakably musical theme.

Gilded Invitations

1. Print party information on the inside of the card. Copy a favorite carol onto parchment paper; tear or cut it into a rectangle, smaller than the card front. Secure the carol to the card front, using craft glue.

2. Draw a treble clef sign on the card front, over the parchment, using dimensional leafing adhesive; follow the manufacturer's directions for drying time.

3. Press gold leaf over the adhesive. Tamp with a firm bristle brush. Brush excess leaf away; fill in empty spaces with leaf flakes.

French Horn Door Swag

What You'll Need

- Fresh or artificial swag
- Medium-size French horn ornament
- Floral paddle wire
- Pinecones; berry stems
- 3 1/2 to 4 yd. (3.2 to 3.7 m) wide ribbon, with musical theme

1. Secure a cluster of pinecones and berry stems to swag at narrowest point, using floral wire. Secure French horn to swag, encircling the cluster, to create a focal point.

2. Form a cluster bow (page 139) with the ribbon, leaving long tails. Secure the bow to the swag above the horn.

Bobeches

Hand-held candles help create the perfect mood, but dripping wax can be a problem. Protect carolers' hands with easy-to-make paper bobeches.

 What You'll Need
- Stiff metallic paper
- Scissors; mat knife
- Ruler; butter knife
- Taper candles

1. Trace the pattern onto stiff metallic paper. Cut out the star. Cut crossed slits in the center to fit the candle.

2. Score the lines that radiate from the center, using a ruler and a butter knife. Alternate from front to back of the star with every line.

3. Fold the star slightly on scored lines, alternating directions as scored. Insert the candle from the right side.

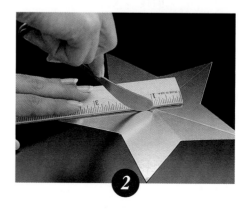

bobeche pattern

Music Folders

Bright Idea

Plan to have carolers sing together in pairs. While one person holds the candle, the other turns the pages, which are all neatly held together in a festive music folder.

You can download Christmas carols from the Internet. Simply search with the term "Christmas carols" to find lyrics for all of your favorites.

Fa-la-la-la-la,....

Scarves

Give the carolers a unified look with warm and wonderful polar fleece scarves. Because the fleece does not ravel, the scarves are a snap to make. Cut 9" (23 cm) strips across the fabric from selvage to selvage. Trim off the selvages, and cut 4" (10 cm) fringe at each end. What a great caroling party memento!

Horn Napkin Rings

Miniature French horns make perfect napkin rings, and nothing could be easier. Add a sprig of holly to make it look like you spent hours making them.

Music Box Place Cards

This precious little gift need never be opened to enjoy it. Inside each neatly wrapped package is a music box movement that plays a favorite Christmas carol.

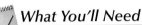

What You'll Need

- Small cardboard box with lid
- Styrofoam® sheets, 1/4" (6 mm) thick
- Mat knife; awl
- Wind-up music box movement
- Wrapping paper; glue; ribbon
- Gift tag

1. Remove the winder from the movement. Insert the movement inside the box.

2. Cut Styrofoam into shapes to fit snugly around the movement, holding it in place. Position the movement so that the winder stem is not in the center.

3. Make a pattern to locate the position of the winder stem. Mark the position on the box lid, and punch a hole with the awl. Put the lid on the box.

4. Wrap the box with wrapping paper, using glue to secure the bottom and ends. Punch a hole through the wrapping paper, aligning it to the hole in the lid. Attach the winder to the stem.

5. Wrap the box with ribbon and tie a bow. Attach a gift tag bearing the guest's name.

Table Swag

This centerpiece is especially suitable if you are able to seat the entire choir, perhaps ten or twelve people, around one long table.

 What You'll Need

- Artificial greenery swag
- Candles
- Miniature musical instruments
- Tiny wrapped boxes
- Wide ribbon with musical theme

1. Arrange the swag in an S shape down the center of the table. Twist the ribbon loosely throughout the garland.

2. Decorate the swag with tiny instruments and wrapped boxes. Nestle candles in the curves of the swag.

Chair Garland

Decorate each chair back with a simple beaded garland, accented at the center with a large clef sign. Add a bow, repeating the ribbon used in the swag.

Bright Idea

Secure garlands to wooden chairs using decorative cord or chenille stems. For chairs with upholstered backs, use twist pins.

recipes

Wassail

Wassail is an old toast from the Norse words, "Ves heill," which mean, "Be in good health."

Yield: 12 cups (3L)

- Peel of 1 lemon
- 3 slices peeled fresh gingerroot
- 1 stick cinnamon
- 1 teaspoon (5 mL) whole allspice
- 6 cups (1.5 L) dry red wine or cranberry juice
- 6 cups (1.5 L) apple cider
- $1/2$ cup (125 mL) sugar
- 2 oranges, unpeeled, cut into 6 wedges each
- 36 whole cloves

Place lemon peel, gingerroot, cinnamon, and allspice on a small piece of cheesecloth or in a paper coffee filter. Bundle up the corners and tie top with kitchen string, leaving excess string to hang out of pot for easy retrieval. Set sachet aside.

In 6-quart (6 L) Dutch oven, combine wine, apple cider, and sugar. Add sachet. Bring to boil over high heat, stirring until sugar is dissolved. Cover. Reduce heat to medium-low. Simmer for 15 minutes. Remove sachet. Keep wassail warm over low heat.

While wassail simmers, stick 3 whole cloves into peel side of each orange wedge. Place one wedge in each serving cup and ladle hot wassail over top. Serve hot.

White Bean-Sundried Tomato Crostini

Yield: 18 to 20 appetizers

- 1 can (15 oz./450 g) cannellini beans, rinsed and drained
- 1 tablespoon (15 mL) white wine vinegar
- 1 tablespoon (15 mL) olive oil
- $1/2$ to 1 teaspoon (2 to 5 mL) minced garlic
- 3 tablespoons (50 mL) finely chopped sundried tomatoes packed in oil, drained
- $1/2$ teaspoon (2 mL) salt
- $1/4$ teaspoon (1 mL) dried thyme leaves
- $1/4$ teaspoon (1 mL) pepper
- 18 to 20 slices French bread
- Chopped fresh parsley

Combine beans, vinegar, oil, and garlic in food processor or blender. Process until smooth, scraping sides of container as necessary. Transfer puree to small bowl. Stir in tomatoes, salt, thyme, and pepper. Cover bean spread and chill at least 2 hours to let flavors blend.

Toast French bread under broiler, 4" (10 cm) from heat, for 2 to 3 minutes per side. Spread 1 heaping tablespoon (15 mL) bean spread on each slice of toast. Garnish with chopped fresh parsley.

Per 2 Pieces: Calories: 197 • Protein: 7 g. • Carbohydrate: 32 g. • Fat: 4 g.
• Cholesterol: 0 mg. • Sodium: 570 mg.
Exchanges: 2 starch, $1/2$ vegetable, $3/4$ fat

Spicy Italian Breadsticks

In large mixing bowl, combine water and yeast, stirring to dissolve yeast. Let stand 5 minutes, until yeast begins to bubble. Stir in oil and salt. Stir in 2 cups (500 mL) flour and beat well. Stir in enough of remaining flour to form dough that pulls away from sides of bowl.

Turn dough onto lightly floured surface. Knead in remaining flour until dough is smooth and elastic, about 8 minutes. Place dough in lightly greased bowl, turning to coat dough. Cover with plastic wrap. Let rise in warm place for 1 to 1½ hours, or until doubled in size. While dough rises, combine seasoning mix ingredients.

Heat oven to 450°F/230°C. Gently pat risen dough into 14" × 4" (35.5 × 10 cm) rectangle, being careful not to deflate the dough. Cut dough crosswise into quarters. Brush tops of quarters evenly with 1 teaspoon (5 mL) olive oil. Sprinkle seasoning mix evenly over top and lightly press seasoning onto dough.

Cut first quarter of dough crosswise into 6 equal pieces. Stretch and roll each piece into an 11" to 12" (28 to 30.5 cm) long strip. (Dough rolls easiest on lightly oiled surface.) Slightly twist each strip, then transfer to baking sheet. Continue making strips from remaining dough quarters.

Bake breadsticks, one pan at a time, for 10 to 12 minutes, or until golden brown. Serve breadsticks the day you make them, as they will get hard overnight.

Per Breadstick: Calories: 80 • Protein: 2 g. • Carbohydrate: 14 g. • Fat: 1 g.
• Cholesterol: 0 mg. • Sodium: 128 mg.
Exchanges: 1 starch

Yield: 24 breadsticks

Dough:
- 1 cup (25 mL) warm water (100°F/37°C)
- 2½ teaspoons (12 mL) active dry yeast
- 2 tablespoons (25 mL) olive oil
- 1 teaspoon (5 mL) salt
- 3½ cups (875 mL) all-purpose flour, divided

Seasoning Mix:
- 1½ teaspoons (7 mL) dried oregano leaves
- 1½ teaspoons (7 mL) dried basil leaves
- 1 teaspoon (5 mL) garlic powder
- ½ to 1 teaspoon (2 to 5 mL) crushed red pepper flakes
- ½ teaspoon (2 mL) fennel seeds
- ½ teaspoon (2 mL) kosher salt
- 1 teaspoon (5 mL) olive oil

Roasted Asparagus

Yield: 12 servings

- 2 lbs. (1 kg) fresh asparagus, trimmed
- 2 tablespoons (25 mL) olive oil
- ½ teaspoon (2 mL) salt
- ½ teaspoon (2 mL) pepper

Dressing:
- ½ cup (125 mL) olive oil
- 2 to 3 tablespoons (25 to 50 mL) white wine vinegar
- 1 teaspoon (5 mL) Dijon mustard
- 1 teaspoon (5 mL) minced garlic
- ½ teaspoon (2 mL) salt

Heat oven to 400°F/200°C. Toss asparagus in 2 tablespoons (25 mL) olive oil to coat. Spread in single layer on large baking sheet. Sprinkle evenly with salt and pepper. Roast asparagus for 10 to 12 minutes, just until tender, turning asparagus over once.

While asparagus roasts, combine dressing ingredients. Whisk well to combine. Drizzle dressing over hot asparagus. Serve immediately.

Per Serving: Calories: 114 • Protein: 2 g. • Carbohydrate: 2 g. • Fat: 11 g.
• Cholesterol: 0 mg. • Sodium: 204 mg.
Exchanges: ½ vegetable, 2¼ fat

Italian-Style Lasagna

Yield: 12 servings

Sauce*:
- 2 tablespoons (25 mL) olive oil
- 1 medium onion, chopped (1 1/2 cups/ 375 mL)
- 1 tablespoon (15 mL) minced garlic
- 2 cans (28 oz./790 g each) diced tomatoes, undrained
- 1/4 cup (60 mL) tomato paste
- 2 teaspoons (10 mL) dried basil
- 2 teaspoons (10 mL) dried oregano
- 1 teaspoon (5 mL) salt
- 1/2 teaspoon (2 mL) pepper

Cheese Filling:
- 1 container (24 oz./680 g) large-curd cottage cheese
- 1 egg
- 1/2 teaspoon (2 mL) salt
- 1/4 teaspoon (1 mL) pepper
- Dash ground nutmeg

- 1 lb. (450 g) ground Italian sausage (mild or spicy)
- 18 sheets oven-ready lasagna noodles, uncooked
- 1 3/4 cups (425 mL) shredded Parmesan cheese
- 1 2/3 cups (400 mL) shredded mozzarella cheese

For sauce, heat olive oil over medium heat. Add onion and garlic. Sauté for 8 to 10 minutes, or until onion is tender. Add remaining sauce ingredients. Bring to a simmer. Reduce heat to medium-low. Simmer for 35 to 45 minutes, or until sauce is thickened and most of the excess liquid has bubbled away. Cool sauce. Process in food processor or through a food mill for a smoother, more uniform texture. Chill several hours or overnight.

For cheese filling, combine cottage cheese, egg, salt, pepper, and nutmeg in food processor or blender. Process until very smooth, scraping sides of container as necessary. Chill several hours or overnight.

Before assembling lasagna, brown sausage in a large skillet over medium heat, making sure to break up sausage chunks into small pieces. Drain sausage and let cool. Set out all ingredients for assembling lasagna.

Spread 1/4 cup (60 mL) sauce in bottom of 9" × 13" (23 × 33 cm) pan. Arrange 3 lasagna noodles crosswise in pan. (They won't cover the bottom of the pan, but will expand during cooking.) Spread 1 heaping tablespoon (15 mL) cheese filling over each noodle. Top noodles with 3/4 cup (175 mL) sauce, one-fifth of the sausage, 1/3 cup (75 mL) mozzarella, and 1/4 cup (59 mL) Parmesan. Repeat these layers four more times, gently pressing down each time you add lasagna noodles. Top with remaining 3 lasagna noodles. Spread 3/4 cup (175 mL) sauce over top and sprinkle remaining 1/2 cup (125 mL) Parmesan evenly over sauce. (There will be some sauce left over. Warm it and serve it over the lasagna, or save it for other uses.)

The assembled lasagna can be covered with plastic and refrigerated for several hours or overnight at this point. To bake, heat oven to 400°F/200°C. Bake uncovered lasagna for 40 to 50 minutes, or until bubbly around edges. Let rest 15 minutes before cutting.

If desired, substitute 4 3/4 cups (1.25 L) jarred marinara sauce for homemade sauce.

Per Serving: Calories: 454 • Protein: 26 g. • Carbohydrate: 33 g. • Fat: 25 g. • Cholesterol: 76 mg. • Sodium: 1,338 mg. Exchanges: 2 3/4 medium-fat meat, 1 1/4 starch, 2 1/2 vegetable, 2 fat

Chocolate Swirl Cheesecake

Yield: 12 servings

- 1 cup (250 mL) chocolate cookie crumbs
- $1/2$ cup (125 mL) ground blanched almonds
- 3 tablespoons (50 mL) sugar
- $1/4$ cup (60 mL) butter, melted
- 2 oz. (60 g) unsweetened chocolate
- 4 pkgs. (8 oz./220 g each) cream cheese, softened
- 1 cup (250 mL) sugar
- 1 teaspoon (5 mL) vanilla extract
- $1/4$ teaspoon (1 mL) almond extract
- 4 eggs

Heat oven to 325°F/160°C. Spray a 9" (23 cm) springform pan with nonstick vegetable cooking spray. Line pan with circle of parchment paper. Spray paper. If pan does not seal tightly, wrap the outside with a wide sheet of foil, coming up the sides of the pan as much as possible. (The pan will bake in a water bath, and you don't want any water to reach the bottom of the pan.) Set aside.

For crust, combine cookie crumbs, almonds, and sugar in a medium mixing bowl. Add butter and stir until combined. Press crumb mixture evenly into bottom of prepared pan. Begin heating water for water bath.

Melt chocolate in double boiler or small saucepan over very low heat, stirring often. Set aside to cool. In large mixing bowl, beat cheese, sugar, vanilla, and almond extract at medium speed of electric mixer until smooth, scraping sides of bowl as necessary. Beat in eggs one at a time.

Place one-third of batter in second bowl. Add melted chocolate to this bowl. Stir to combine. Alternately spoon large scoops of white batter and small scoops of chocolate batter into prepared pan. Swirl batters together with a knife.

Place springform pan in roasting pan. Set in oven then fill roaster with hot water until it comes $1/3$ up sides of springform pan. (Don't let water get inside foil wrap.) Bake $1\frac{1}{4}$ to $1\frac{1}{2}$ hours, or until cake is set around the edges and slightly jiggly in center. Place springform pan on cooling rack. Run a sharp

knife around edge of cake, but don't loosen sides of pan. Cool completely. Refrigerate for several hours or overnight.

Remove sides from pan. Invert a plate lightly on top of cake and flip everything over. Remove bottom of pan and parchment from bottom of cake. Invert serving plate on bottom of cake and flip everything over again. Remove first plate. Garnish cake as desired and serve.

Per Serving: Calories: 489 • Protein: 10 g. • Carbohydrate: 31 g. • Fat: 38 g.
• Cholesterol: 165 mg. • Sodium: 339 mg.
Exchanges: 1 medium-fat meat, 1 starch, 6 fat, 1 other carbohydrate

Open House Buffet

An open house celebration gives neighbors and friends the chance to drop by and exchange their seasonal greetings. Decked out in wall-to-wall Christmas, your home is a spirited expression of holiday hospitality.

— Menu —

Buttered Rum Cashews

Mocha Eggnog

Cheddar and Apple Cider Fondue

Shrimp with Sweet-Spicy BBQ Sauce

Seasoned Pita Chips with Bean Dip

Artichoke-Beef Tarts

With careful planning and advance preparation, you can free yourself up to enjoy the party and spend a few minutes with every guest. Make-ahead foods set out on a help-yourself buffet need little attention from the host. With paper plates and napkins and plastic cups and utensils that also mean easy cleanup, you're prepared for a crowd. Separate small buffet tables for beverages, hearty appetizers, finger snacks, and desserts encourage guests to mingle.

Make your home a holiday haven with lavish decorations, glowing candles, merry music, and a warm fire. Take this opportunity to showcase your Christmas collections or a selection of framed photos from Christmases past. Then unify your decorating plan by repeating a design element, like red and green Christmas plaids, from the front door to the buffet tables.

Open Door Invitations

What You'll Need

- Single-fold invitations or card stock, cut and folded
- Computer (optional)
- Light-colored paper
- Glue
- Preserved cedar
- Mat knife
- Confetti; ribbon; gold cord
- Envelopes

1. Print the party information on the inside of the card. Draw a rectangle on the front to represent a door. Glue a small sprig of greenery and a tiny ribbon bow to the upper half of the door. Open the card. Using the mat knife, cut along three sides of the door, leaving it hinged on the fourth side.

2. Cut a sheet of light-colored paper to fit the inside of the card front. Glue it in place behind the door. Cut a tip from a preserved cedar branch for a tree, and glue it to the paper behind the door. Glue thin gold cord garland and confetti ornaments to the tree.

Lit Grapevine Tree

Greet friends and neighbors with a cheerful lit grapevine tree, placed by your front door. While illuminating the front step, its jaunty plaid ribbon introduces your design theme.

What You'll Need
- Grapevine tree form
- Single string of 100 lights
- Plaid ribbon
- Wire twist ties
- Urn or planter

1. Feed the first light of the string (opposite the plug end) up inside the tree from the bottom. Bring it out in an opening near the tree top. Bring the next four lights out through the opening, leaving the wires inside the tree. Cluster the lights and secure them to the vine, using a twist tie.

2. Repeat step 1 with the next five lights clustered in a nearby opening. Continue in this manner, spiralling downward, for a total of twenty light clusters. Feed the remaining cord out through the bottom of the tree. Wrap the tree with ribbon and wire a cluster bow (page 139) to the top. "Plant" the tree in an urn or planter near the front door.

Luminary Walkway

Light the way to your front door with glowing luminaries. Quick and easy to make, these luminaries are simply glass quart canning jars tied up with plaid ribbons. Candles secured to the jar bottoms with floral putty can be tipped for easy lighting.

Santa Sleigh Accent

Fill a napkin-lined sleigh with wrapped chocolates as a good-cheer accompaniment to a welcoming cup of mocha eggnog (page 74).

Mantel Cloth

Assemble a mantel cloth from overlapping plaid napkins. Use the space to display a nativity scene or a collection of Christmas artwork or memorabilia.

What You'll Need

- Dinner napkins in plaids and solid colors
- Narrow wired ribbon
- Medium-size jingle bells (or small ornaments)
- Small safety pins
- Double-stick tape

1. Arrange napkins on the mantel with points hanging down. Overlap and adjust placement to cover the entire mantel. Pin the layers together temporarily. Secure with double-stick tape or safety pins, inserted from the underside. Turn under the napkins at the back of the mantel.

2. Tie a small wired ribbon bow for each napkin point. Hand-stitch a small bell or ornament and a bow to each point.

3. Secure the arrangement to the mantel, using double-stick tape.

Buffet Table Drapery

Set up an impressive buffet table in a matter of minutes. Gather a selection of various items to use as risers for the serving pieces and centerpiece of the main buffet table. Include inverted cake pans, sturdy boxes, and inverted wide clay pot saucers, which work well for hot food items. Arrange the risers on the table, over a plaid tablecloth. Drape a length of festive glossy gold fabric over the risers. Tucking the raw edges under, swaddle and arrange the fabric casually over the table surface.

Collection Centerpiece

Take advantage of the center of a walk-around buffet to show off a treasured collection. On the central riser, spread a bed of fresh pine boughs or seeded eucalyptus branches. Then arrange your prized nut-crackers and smokers, a flock of Christmas angels, a village of porcelain houses, or a cast of Santa Claus figures.

Woven Heart Napkin Caddy

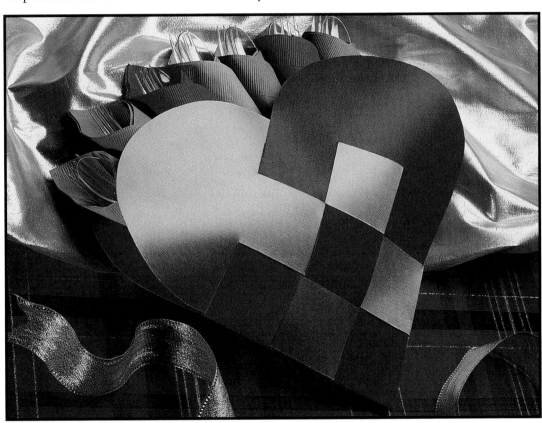

For your guests' convenience, wrap paper napkins around plastic flatware to be dispensed from a satin woven heart caddy at the end of the buffet line.

Bright Idea

If you decide to move the dining room table against a wall for the buffet, be sure to raise the chandelier above head level.

What You'll Need

- 1/4 yd. (0.25 m) each of gold and red glossy fabric, such as satin
- 1/2 yd. (0.5 m) fusible web, such as Wonder-Under®

1. Fuse the fabrics, wrong sides together, following the manufacturer's directions. Cut two 22" × 6¾" (56 × 17 cm) rectangles of the fused fabric.

2. Press the rectangles in half, crosswise, one

with red side out and the other gold. Starting from the fold, mark two cutting lines 2¼" (6 cm) from the edges and 7" (18 cm) long; cut.

3. Leading with the fold, weave the first gold loop alternately through and around the red loops. Snug the loop up to the end of the slits. Weave the second loop in the opposite order, and the third loop in the same order as the first. Round the corners of the open ends to form a heart.

71

Placemat Basket

Fashion a basket for the buffet from a purchased plaid placemat. Use it to hold rolls or cookies. Or design it to fit snugly around a 9" × 13" (23 × 33 cm) pan.

What You'll Need
- Plaid placemat
- Awl
- Darning needle
- Narrow ribbon

1. Fold in the sides and ends of the placemat an even distance all around and pin. If desired to fit a specific pan, pin the placemat snugly around the pan. Press creases in the placemat to form a flat bottom.

2. At the point where a side and end meet, about ¼" (6 mm) below the edge, form holes through the placemat, using an awl. Thread a darning needle with the narrow ribbon and run the needle through the placemat. Knot the ribbon and tie a bow. Repeat for each corner.

Guest Book

Give yourself a lasting memento of the party with a guest book, signed by all of your visitors. Decorate the front of a blank journal book and place it conveniently on an end table where everyone can take a turn writing out their holiday wishes. Designate some pages for photographs if you wish to take party pictures and insert them later.

Parting Favors

Fill cellophane bags with Buttered Rum Cashews (page 74) or your favorite Christmas treat and tie them closed with ribbon. Put them in a gilded basket tied up with a large plaid bow set near the front door, so parting guests can take one as they leave.

Buttered Rum Cashews

Yield: 4 cups (1 L)

- $3/4$ cup (175 mL) butter
- $2/3$ cup (150 mL) sugar
- $1/3$ cup (75 mL) light corn syrup
- 5 tablespoons (75 mL) dark rum (or $1/4$ cup/60 mL water plus 1 tablespoon/15 mL rum extract)
- 4 cups (1 L) whole roasted cashews or assorted nuts

In medium saucepan, melt butter over medium heat. Stir in sugar, corn syrup, and rum. Cook for 35 to 40 minutes, or until candy thermometer reads 275°F/135°C (soft-crack stage), stirring occasionally.

Add cashews, stirring gently to coat. Spread mixture on lightly oiled baking sheet to cool and dry. Break up nuts after drying to form small clumps. Store in airtight container.

Note: These are buttery nuts, so if packaging as gifts, place them in plastic bags instead of paper.

Per $1/4$ Cup (60 mL): Calories: 334 • Protein: 5 g. • Carbohydrate: 25 g. • Fat: 24 g.
• Cholesterol: 23 mg. • Sodium: 102 mg.
Exchanges: $3/4$ high-fat meat, $33/4$ fat, $11/2$ other carbohydrate

Mocha Eggnog

Yield: 9 cups (2.25 L)

- $11/2$ cups (375 mL) hot water*
- 3 tablespoons (50 mL) instant espresso powder*
- 2 cartons (32 oz./1L each) eggnog
- 1 cup (250 mL) chocolate syrup
- Whipped cream
- Candied espresso beans, crushed

Combine water and espresso powder. Stir to dissolve powder. Let cool. In large container, combine cooled espresso, eggnog, and syrup. Cover and chill. Stir just before serving. Garnish individual servings with a dollop of whipped cream topped with a sprinkling of crushed espresso beans.

*You may substitute $11/2$ cups (375 mL) strong coffee for the water and espresso powder.

Note: This recipe multiplies easily.

Per $1/2$ Cup (125 mL): Calories: 190 • Protein: 5 g. • Carbohydrate: 25 g. • Fat: 9 g.
• Cholesterol: 67 mg. • Sodium: 77 mg.
Exchanges: $1/2$ whole milk, 1 fat, $11/3$ other carbohydrate

Cheddar and Apple Cider Fondue

Yield: 2 cups (500 mL)

- ½ cup (125 mL) high-quality apple cider
- ½ cup (125 mL) dry white wine
- 2 tablespoons (25 mL) lemon juice
- 1 lb. (450 g) smoked Cheddar cheese, shredded (about 6 cups/1.5 L)

- 4 teaspoons (20 mL) cornstarch
- ¼ teaspoon (1 mL) ground nutmeg
- ¼ teaspoon (1 mL) freshly ground pepper
- Dippers: apple or pear slices, breadsticks, cubed pumpernickel bread, cubed summer sausage

In medium saucepan, heat cider, wine, and lemon juice to a simmer. In sealable plastic bag, toss cheese and cornstarch until cheese is evenly coated. Add cheese to cider mixture a handful at a time, whisking until cheese is melted before adding more. Stir in nutmeg and pepper.

Transfer fondue to a fondue pot or slow-cooker to keep warm. Stir occasionally while fondue sits.

Notes: For best quality, make single batches of fondue, then combine them in a large slow-cooker for serving.

If fondue appears grainy after whisking in cheese, whisk in another 1 tablespoon (15 mL) lemon juice.

A slow-cooker is best for serving fondue if it sits for a long time. It requires less attention than a fondue pot as its heat is more gentle.

Per ¼ Cup (60 mL): Calories: 252 • Protein: 14 g. • Carbohydrate: 4 g. • Fat: 19 g.
• Cholesterol: 60 mg. • Sodium: 354 mg.
Exchanges: 2 high-fat meat, ½ fat, ¼ other carbohydrate

Chilled Shrimp with Sweet-Spicy BBQ Sauce

Yield: 10 servings

Sauce:
- 1 cup (250 mL) chili sauce
- 1 cup (250 mL) ketchup
- ½ cup (125 mL) honey
- 2 tablespoons (25 mL) dry mustard
- 2 tablespoons (25 mL) prepared horseradish
- 1 tablespoon (15 mL) Worcestershire sauce

- 1 tablespoon (15 mL) hot red pepper sauce
- 1 teaspoon (5 mL) minced garlic

- 2 lbs. (1 kg) medium shrimp (30 to 35 count), cooked, shelled, and deveined (tails on), chilled

In medium mixing bowl, combine sauce ingredients. (Sauce can be made several days in advance and refrigerated in covered container.) Serve sauce with shrimp.

Per Serving: Calories: 191 • Protein: 16 g. • Carbohydrate: 29 g. • Fat: 2 g.
• Cholesterol: 112 mg. • Sodium: 818 mg.
Exchanges: 2 very lean meat, ¼ fat, 1¾ other carbohydrate

Seasoned Pita Chips with Bean Dip

Yield: 10 servings

Pita Chips:
- 6 pocket pita breads
- $3/4$ cup (175 mL) olive oil
- 2 teaspoons (10 mL) chili powder
- 1 teaspoon (5 mL) ground cumin
- $1/2$ teaspoon (2 mL) garlic powder
- $1/2$ teaspoon (2 mL) salt
- $1/4$ teaspoon (1 mL) cayenne pepper

Bean Dip:
- 2 cans (15 oz./425 g each) cannellini beans*, rinsed and drained
- 2 tablespoons (25 mL) lime juice
- 1 tablespoon (15 mL) olive oil
- $1/2$ cup (125 mL) finely chopped red bell pepper
- $1/4$ cup (60 mL) chopped fresh cilantro leaves
- 1 jalapeño pepper, seeded and finely chopped
- 1 teaspoon (5 mL) chili powder
- $1/2$ teaspoon (2 mL) ground cumin
- $1/2$ teaspoon (2 mL) salt
- $1/2$ teaspoon (2 mL) hot red pepper sauce (optional)

Heat oven to 375°F/190°C. Cut pita breads apart to form two rounds. In small bowl, combine remaining pita chip ingredients. Brush cut sides of pita rounds with seasoned oil mixture. Using a pizza cutter or large knife, cut each round into six wedges. Arrange wedges on large baking sheets. Bake one sheet at a time for 7 to 9 minutes, or until chips are crisp.

For bean dip, combine beans, lime juice, and olive oil in food processor or blender. Process until smooth, scraping sides of container as necessary. In medium mixing bowl, combine pureed beans and remaining bean dip ingredients. Cover with plastic wrap and chill at least 1 hour to allow flavors to blend.

You may substitute navy or great Northern beans for cannellini beans, but they won't be as smooth and creamy when pureed.

Note: The chips are at their best if served soon after making them. However, they can be made a day ahead and stored in a sealable plastic bag. Refresh them by spreading them on a baking sheet and baking at 350°F/180°C for 5 minutes before serving.

Per Serving: Calories: 321 • Protein: 8 g. • Carbohydrate: 31 g. • Fat: 19 g. • Cholesterol: 0 mg. • Sodium: 539 mg. Exchanges: 2 starch, $3^1/2$ fat

Artichoke-Beef Tarts

Yield: 36 tarts

Crusts:
- 1½ cups (375 mL) all-purpose flour
- 2 tablespoons (25 mL) grated Parmesan cheese
- ¼ teaspoon (1 mL) salt
- 6 tablespoons (85 mL) butter, chilled and cubed
- 1 egg beaten with 2 tablespoons (25 mL) water

Filling:
- 1 container (8 oz./227 g) herbed cream cheese, softened
- 1 tablespoon (15 mL) cream or milk

Topping:
- 4 oz. (114 g) deli-style roast beef
- 1 jar (6½ oz./184 g) marinated artichoke hearts, drained
- 5 cherry tomatoes

For tart crusts, combine flour, Parmesan, and salt in a food processor. Add butter, and pulse until mixture resembles coarse cornmeal. With motor running, add beaten egg in slow drizzle until dough clings and forms into a ball. (If necessary, drizzle in an additional tablespoon [15 mL] of cold water.) Press dough into a ball and wrap with plastic wrap. Flatten dough into a disk. Chill for at least 30 minutes.

Heat oven to 400°F/200°C. Roll dough to ⅛" (3 mm) thickness. Use a 2½" (6.5 cm) round cutter to cut dough into rounds. (It may be necessary to roll half of the dough at a time and reroll any scraps.) Fit dough circles into ungreased mini-muffin tins. Prick the bottom of crusts with fork. Bake for 8 to 10 minutes, or until crusts are golden brown. (Crusts may be made several days ahead and stored in an airtight container.)

For filling, stir cream cheese and cream together until smooth. Spoon a heaping teaspoon of filling into each tart crust. Cut roast beef into 1" (2.5 cm) strips. Roll strips into short cylinders and place one end in filling. Cut artichoke hearts into small pieces and add a piece to each tart. Finally, cut tomatoes into thin wedges and add a wedge to each tart. (Tarts may be assembled a couple of hours before serving. Cover with plastic and refrigerate until ready to serve.)

Note: Create a platter of assorted tarts with the following topping options:
—Smoked salmon and pickled asparagus spears
—Rolled deli-sliced ham and cornichon pickle spears
—Cured Italian meats (coppacola, salami, prosciutto), pepperoncini peppers, and kalamata olives

Per 2 Tarts: Calories: 143 • Protein: 4 g. • Carbohydrate: 10 g. • Fat: 10 g. • Cholesterol: 38 mg. • Sodium: 247 mg.
Exchanges: ¼ lean meat, ½ starch, ½ vegetable, 1¾ fat

Christmas Tea

Rich in the tradition and romance of the Victorian era, a holiday tea celebrates the season in a uniquely festive way. Lush fragrant rose bouquets, elegant table decor, and a proper cup of tea embody the aura of old Britain.

Menu

The Perfect Cup of Tea

Assorted Finger Sandwiches

Lace Cookie Flutes

Mini Pavlovas

Sacher Torte Squares

Take this opportunity to be prim and proper in every aspect of the party, from the dainty raised embossing on the invitations to the exquisite tea cakes and finger sandwiches served on doily-covered china serving pieces. Set your table with a variety of fine china place settings collected from friends or purchased as odds and ends at estate sales. Add romantic richness to the party setting with lavish fresh floral decorations, especially welcome in areas where gardens are tucked away for the winter. With strict attention to details, ceremoniously prepare and serve a proper pot of tea, and treat your guests like royalty with individually appointed bud vases and hand-made Victorian lace nosegays.

Heat Embossed Invitations

Stamp and emboss intricate looking invitations using a rubber stamp teacup image. With your delicate personal touch, stir the expectations of your guests.

What You'll Need

- Blank cards with envelopes
- Scissors with deckle-blades
- Decorative papers; card stock
- Rubber stamp of a teacup or teapot image
- Embossing ink
- Embossing powder
- Heat gun or small table lamp
- Watercolor pencils or pastels
- Glue

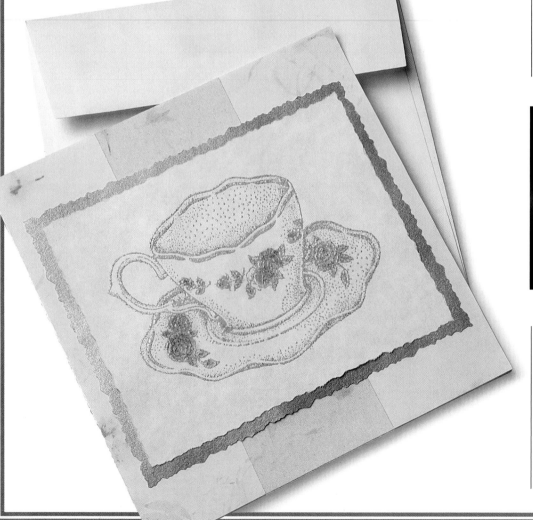

1. Write party information on the inside of the invitation. Stamp a teacup design on card stock, using embossing ink. Immediately sprinkle the wet ink with embossing powder; shake off the excess powder.

2. Hold the design just above a hot light bulb or heat the embossing powder with a heat gun until the powder melts, forming a raised design. Allow the embossed design to cool completely.

3. Color the desired areas of the design using colored pencils or pastels. Trim around design using scissors with deckle blades. Layer over decorative paper and glue to card front.

Victorian Tree Ornaments

Decorate your Christmas tree with antique teaspoons and tiny porcelain teacups tied up securely with ribbons. Fill in with other Victorian decorations, featuring cherubs, lace, flowers, and lots of ribbon.

Floral Garland

Accent artificial or natural greenery garland with artificial or preserved rose blossoms, baby's breath, and ribbon. Arrange a garland over the fireplace mantel or hang garlands in doorways and along stairway banisters.

Door Bouquet

A lovely hint of what's in store for them greets your guests at the front door. This bouquet of everlasting flowers is held in a cone covered with richly textured anaglyptic wallpaper and laced with ribbon.

What You'll Need

- Styrofoam® cone, 12″ (30.5 cm) high
- Anaglyptic wallpaper, about 2′ × 2′ (61 × 61 cm)
- 1/2 yd. (0.5 m) pregathered lace
- Artificial flowers and greenery
- Ribbon
- Floral pins; hot glue gun

1. Roll the paper around the cone. Trim to fit, overlapping edges in the back. Hot-glue edges together. Trim paper around the top even with the flat end of the cone.

2. Secure pregathered lace around the outer edge of the cone top, inserting floral pins through the lace into the Styrofoam. Trim off and butt the lace ends at the back; allow the lace to hang down over the upper edge of the cone.

3. Cut flower stems to about 6" (15 cm); trim off leaves from lower part of stems. Insert flower stems into cone, working from the center outward. Fill in with greenery stems.

4. Wrap ribbon around the cone as

shown. Secure at the back, using hot glue or floral pin. Secure a ribbon hanging loop at the back of the cone near the upper edge, using floral pins. Insert the pins into the foam, angling slightly upward.

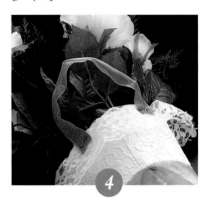

Tablecloths

Layer a crisp white tablecloth over a floral or solid color tablecloth, preferably on a round table. If you are using a square table, turn the white tablecloth so the points hang over the sides. For a rectangular table, use two overlapping square white tablecloths. Gather up the points of the white tablecloth with rubber bands. Then tie fresh or artificial flowers and greens over the rubber bands with lush ribbon bows.

Napkin Roses

Roll each cloth napkin into the shape of a rose, following the diagrams below. Tie them with green velvet ribbons and place one gracefully across each plate.

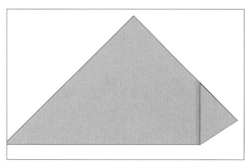

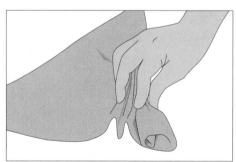

1. Fold in half diagonally, right side out, with fold at bottom. Turn lower right corner up at right angle to fold.

2. Scrunch and roll napkin from right to left, about 3" (7.5 cm) from fold, forming rose. Tie tightly with ribbon.

Bright Idea

To remove candle wax from fabric, first scrape away the excess. Stretch the fabric taut, right side down, over a deep pot, securing the fabric to the pot with a rubber band. From 12" (30.5 cm) above the cloth, pour boiling water over the spot.

Chair Covers

Sew small tassels or crystals to the corners of large dinner napkins, and place them diagonally over the chair seats and backs.

Place Card Cordials

Use cordial glasses as tiny vases to hold individual rose buds for each guest. Print names on embossed place cards at the base of each one.

Teapot Centerpiece

Create a fresh floral arrangement around an ornate china teapot as an eyecatching centerpiece. Insert cut stems into individual water tubes for lasting freshness. See page 136 for more tips on arranging fresh flowers.

Surround the centerpiece with mix'n'match teacups filled with floating candles. Candlelight and flowers are the perfect complements for each other.

Nosegay Favors

As a memento of your holiday tea party, favor each guest with a personal lacy nosegay. Filled with lightly scented potpourri, it can be used as a pomander or a tree ornament.

What You'll Need

- 6" (15 cm) doilies, one for each nosegay
- 6" (15 cm) tulle circle, available in bridal departments of fabric and craft stores; one for each nosegay
- Needle and thread
- Narrow ribbon, two 10" (25.5 cm) pieces for each nosegay
- Two ribbon rosebuds
- Lightly scented potpourri
- Dried rosebuds
- Hot glue gun

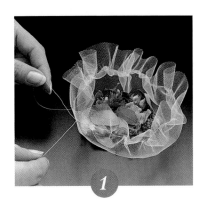

1. Run a gathering stitch around the tulle circle, 1" (2.5 cm) from the outer edge. Place a small amount of potpourri in the center of the tulle circle. Pull up on the gathering thread and tie, forming a loose bag.

2. Roll the doily into a cone shape, overlapping the edges in front or back. Secure with a few small hand stitches.

Insert the potpourri bag, allowing the gathered edge to fan out at the opening of the cone.

3. Hot-glue dried rosebuds to center of fanned tulle. Hand-stitch a ribbon handle to each side of the cone. Stitch or glue ribbon rosebuds at the points of attachment. Tie the handles together in a bow above the cone.

The Perfect Cup of Tea

There are three basic types of tea: Green—the most delicate; oolong—moderate flavor and color; and black—the strongest flavor and darkest color of the teas. Black teas, such as Earl Grey, English Breakfast, or Irish Breakfast, are the most popular in the U.S., and they are the best choice for an afternoon Christmas Tea. Loose-leaf teas are better than tea bags for brewing a pot of tea.

To make a pot of tea, bring a kettle of water to a rolling boil. Swirl a little hot water in a teapot to warm it, then

Finger Sandwiches

Roast Beef and Avocado
Yield: 12 finger sandwiches

- 6 slices multigrain bread
- 1/4 cup (60 mL) butter, softened
- 4 oz. (114 g) deli-sliced roast beef
- 2 avocados, peeled, pitted, and sliced
- 1/2 cup (125 mL) thinly sliced radishes

Cut the crusts off the bread. Spread butter evenly on slices of bread. Top three slices evenly with roast beef, avocado slices, and radishes. Top with remaining slices of bread. Cut each sandwich crosswise into four rectangles.

Per 2 Sandwiches: Calories: 264 • Protein: 8 g.
• Carbohydrate: 17 g. • Fat: 20 g. • Cholesterol: 29 mg.
• Sodium: 404 mg.
Exchanges: 1/2 lean meat, 1 starch, 1/2 vegetable, 3 1/2 fat

Walnut Chicken Salad
Yield: 12 finger sandwiches

- 8 oz. (227 g) boneless, skinless chicken breast, cooked, finely chopped
- 1/4 cup (60 mL) shredded carrot
- 1/4 cup (60 mL) golden raisins
- 1/4 cup (60 mL) chopped walnuts
- 4 to 5 tablespoons (60 to 75 mL) mayonnaise
- 1/2 teaspoon (2 mL) curry powder (optional)
- 6 slices white bread
- 1 bunch watercress, stems removed

In medium mixing bowl, combine chicken, carrot, raisins, and walnuts. Add mayonnaise and curry powder; mix well. Cover with plastic wrap and chill for at least one hour to allow flavors to blend.

Cut the crusts off the bread. Spread chicken salad evenly on three slices of bread. Top evenly with watercress. Top with remaining slices of bread. Cut each sandwich diagonally into four triangles.

Per 2 Sandwiches: Calories: 260 • Protein: 16 g. • Carbohydrate: 19 g. • Fat: 14 g. • Cholesterol: 38 mg. • Sodium: 238 mg.
Exchanges: 1 1/2 very lean meat, 1 starch, 1/4 vegetable, 1/4 fruit, 2 1/2 fat

discard the water. Add tea leaves to pot (one heaping teaspoon [5 mL] per cup plus one extra for the pot). Pour boiling water over the leaves, stir, and cover. Let tea steep for 5 to 7 minutes. To serve, pour the tea through a small fine-mesh strainer. (Alternately, you

may place tea leaves in a tea ball before adding to the pot, but the tea won't brew as strongly since the water can't flow around the leaves.)

Serve tea with milk, lemon slices, sugar, and honey.

Goat Cheese and Marmalade Squares
Yield: 12 finger sandwiches

- 6 slices multigrain bread
- 3 oz. (85 g) goat cheese, softened
- $1/3$ cup (75 mL) orange marmalade

Cut the crusts off the bread. Spread goat cheese evenly on three slices of bread. Top evenly with marmalade. Top with remaining slices of bread. Cut each sandwich into four squares.

Per 2 Sandwiches: Calories: 157 • Protein: 6 g. • Carbohydrate: 24 g. • Fat: 5 g. • Cholesterol: 11 mg. • Sodium: 207 mg.
Exchanges: $1/3$ high-fat meat, 1 starch, $1/3$ fat, $1/2$ other carbohydrate

Turkey and Brie with Cranberry Chutney
Yield: 12 finger sandwiches

- 6 slices white bread
- $1/2$ cup (125 mL) cranberry chutney*
- 4 oz. (114 g) deli-sliced smoked turkey breast
- 6 oz. (170 g) Brie cheese, sliced
- 3 large leaves butter lettuce

Cut the crusts off the bread. Spread chutney evenly on three slices of bread. Top evenly with turkey, Brie, and lettuce. Top with remaining slices of bread. Cut each sandwich crosswise into four rectangles.

If you can't find cranberry chutney, a cranberry relish will work. Or use tangy apricot preserves.

Per 2 Sandwiches: Calories: 266 • Protein: 12 g. • Carbohydrate: 32 g. • Fat: 9 g. • Cholesterol: 37 mg. • Sodium: 720 mg.
Exchanges: $1 1/4$ medium-fat meat, 1 starch, $1/3$ fruit, $1/2$ fat, $3/4$ other carbohydrate

Lace Cookie Flutes

Yield: 20 cookies

- 5 tablespoons (75 mL) butter
- $1/2$ cup (125 mL) light brown sugar
- 2 tablespoons (25 mL) light corn syrup
- $1/8$ teaspoon (0.5 mL) salt
- 1 cup (250 mL) uncooked quick-cooking oats
- 1 tablespoon (15 mL) all-purpose flour
- 1 teaspoon (5 mL) vanilla extract
- $1/2$ cup (125 mL) finely ground blanched almonds

Cinnamon Cream:
- 1 cup (250 mL) heavy cream
- 3 tablespoons (50 mL) powdered sugar
- 1 teaspoon (5 mL) ground cinnamon
- 1 teaspoon (5 mL) vanilla extract

Heat oven to 375°F/190°C. Line baking sheets with parchment paper. In medium saucepan, melt butter over medium heat. Reduce heat to medium-low and simmer for 4 minutes. Stir in sugar, corn syrup, and salt. Cook and stir for 1 to 2 minutes, or just until blended and sugar is dissolved. Remove from heat.

Stir in oats, flour, and vanilla. Fold in almonds. Drop batter by heaping teaspoons (5 mL) onto prepared baking sheets. Leave 4 inches (10 cm) between cookies. Bake one sheet at a time for 8 to 10 minutes, or until cookies are browned and set. Cool for 1 minute on baking sheet.

To make flutes, drape a warm cookie over the round handle of a wooden spoon or pastry brush. Roll ends toward each other to make a loose tube. Press outside edge of cookie against tube. Gently slide cooled cookie off handle. (If cookies harden on the pan before they can be shaped, return them to the oven for 1 minute to soften.) Store unfilled cookies in airtight container.

For Cinnamon Cream, combine cream, sugar, cinnamon, and vanilla in medium mixing bowl. Beat at medium speed of electric mixer just until stiff peaks form. Spoon cream into a pastry bag or sealable plastic bag with a snipped corner. Pipe cream into lace cookie flutes. If desired, drizzle melted chocolate on cookies for decoration.

Note: Don't fill cookies until a couple of hours before serving them. Filled cookies will soften over time.

Per Cookie: Calories: 130 • Protein: 1 g. • Carbohydrate: 12 g. • Fat: 9 g. • Cholesterol: 24 mg. • Sodium: 54 mg.
Exchanges: $1/2$ starch, $13/4$ fat, $1/4$ other carbohydrate

Mini Pavlovas

Yield: 10 Pavlovas

- 3 egg whites, room temperature
- $1/4$ teaspoon (1 mL) cream of tartar
- $1/4$ teaspoon (1 mL) vanilla extract
- $3/4$ cup (175 mL) sugar
- $2^{1/2}$ cups (625 mL) assorted fresh fruit, finely chopped or thinly sliced
- 2 tablespoons (25 mL) orange-flavored liqueur, or 1 tablespoon (15 mL) orange juice concentrate
- 2 tablespoons (25 mL) sugar
- Whipped cream (optional)

Heat oven to 225°F/110°C. Line large baking sheet with parchment paper. Trace ten $2^{1/2}$" (6.5 cm) circles on paper. Turn paper over so you can see tracing, but ink or pencil lead won't get on meringues. Set aside.

In large mixing bowl, combine egg whites, cream of tartar, and vanilla. Beat at high speed of electric mixer until soft peaks begin to form. Continue beating and add sugar, 1 tablespoon (15 mL) at a time. Beat until mixture is thick and glossy.

Spread mixture evenly over circles on prepared baking sheet, mounding slightly around edges. Bake for $1^{1/2}$ hours. Turn oven off. Let meringues cool in closed oven for 1 hour. Remove from oven and cool completely. Store in airtight container for up to a week.

In medium bowl, combine fruit, liqueur, and sugar. Let stand at room temperature for 1 hour. Just before serving, spoon fruit mixture into meringues. Top with a dollop of whipped cream, if desired.

Per Pavlova: Calories: 97 • Protein: 1 g. • Carbohydrate: 22 g.
• Fat: <1 g. • Cholesterol: 0 mg. • Sodium: 17 mg.
Exchanges: 1/4 fruit, 1 1/4 other carbohydrate

Sacher Torte Squares

Yield: 24 squares

- 1 box (1 lb. 2.25 oz./517 g) chocolate cake mix
- 12 oz. (340 g) semisweet chocolate, chopped
- 1 cup (250 mL) heavy cream
- 3 tablespoons (50 mL) butter
- 1 cup (250 mL) apricot preserves

Heat oven to 350°F/180°C. Grease and flour a 10" × 15" (25.5 × 38 cm) baking pan. Prepare cake batter as directed on package. Pour into prepared pan. Bake for 25 to 30 minutes, or until wooden pick inserted in center comes out clean. Turn cake onto cooling rack. Cool completely.

Cut cake in half crosswise. Level cake halves to $3/4$" (2 cm) thickness with serrated knife. Trim edges of cakes so they are straight. Wrap cakes in plastic wrap or foil. Freeze for at least one hour. (Cakes can be well-wrapped and frozen a week or two in advance, too.)

Place chopped chocolate in a medium mixing bowl. In a saucepan, heat cream and butter over medium heat until butter melts and mixture starts to simmer. Pour hot mixture over chocolate. Whisk until chocolate is melted and smooth. Set ganache aside.

Remove cakes from freezer. Spread preserves evenly over top of one cake half. Top with second cake half. Cut layered cake into $1^{1/2}$" (3.8 cm) squares. Arrange squares on waxed paper-lined baking sheets. Spoon warm ganache over each square, letting it drip down sides. Refrigerate until ganache is set. Store squares in single layer in airtight containers.

Per 2 Squares: Calories: 296 • Protein: 3 g. • Carbohydrate: 35 g. • Fat: 17 g.
• Cholesterol: 44 mg. • Sodium: 213 mg.
Exchanges: 1 starch, 3 1/4 fat, 1 1/4 other carbohydrate

Cookie Exchange

Baking is more fun when you can share the cookies with your friends. Early in the holiday season, a cookie exchange party gives everyone a welcome break from busy schedules and sends them home well-stocked for the entertaining season ahead.

Menu

Coffee Bar

Sweet and Spicy Mixed Nuts

Hot Artichoke Ricotta Dip

Herb and Cheese Biscuit Sandwiches

Raspberry Stars

Sugar Plums

Chocolate-Dipped Hazelnut Biscotti

Invite a circle of close friends for a weekend morning filled with laughter, sharing, and indulgent treats. Ask each guest to bake one type of Christmas cookie; one dozen for each of the other guests, packaged in individually wrapped containers and a few extra cookies to share at the party. Decorate with the holiday baking theme in mind, using miniature cookie cutters and doll-size baking utensils found in toy shops or antique stores. Encourage a casual atmosphere with a self-serve coffee bar, stocked with assorted Christmas mugs. Set up a small snack buffet on the living room coffee table with a few simple snacks to complement the real stars of the show—the cookies. Then sit back and enjoy a relaxed atmosphere in the company of special friends.

Recipe Booklet Invitations

This invitation serves both as an announcement of the occasion and a treasured remembrance for each guest. It may even become a tradition, as you gather recipe booklets from cookie exchanges year after year.

What You'll Need

- Blank cards and envelopes slightly larger than recipe card
- Recipe cards; enough for guests and host plus one for each invitation
- Paper punch
- 1/8" (3 mm) ribbon, 3/4 yd. (0.7m) for each booklet

1. Punch holes in the card cover fold, 1" (2.5 cm) from each end. Decorate the front of the cover.

2. Print the party information and instructions for the cookie exchange on a recipe card. Punch holes in the printed card and additional blank recipe cards, 1/4" (6 mm) from the upper edges and aligned to the holes in the cover. Place the cards, with instructions on top, into the cover and into the envelope.

3. At the party, after exchanging recipe cards, give every guest 3/4 yd. (0.7 m) narrow ribbon. Stack the recipe cards and assemble the booklet as shown.

Bright Idea

Store your gingerbread chain in a sealed plastic bag to retain the scent year after year.

Scented Gingerbread Welcome

Hanging in an entryway or over a foyer mirror, this merry chain of scented gingerbread men greets your fellow cookie bakers. The following recipe provides enough "dough" for about eight 4" (10 cm) ornaments. Remember, they're really cute but not edible!

What You'll Need

- 1 cup (250 mL) ground cinnamon
- 1 tablespoon (15 mL) ground cloves
- 1 tablespoon (15 mL) ground nutmeg
- 3/4 cup (175 mL) smooth applesauce
- 2 tablespoons (25 mL) white craft glue
- Gingerbread man cookie cutter, about 4" (10 cm) tall
- Drinking straw
- Small red buttons
- Small black beads for eyes
- White paint pen
- Red gingham ribbon, 1/2" (1.3 cm) wide; 2 yd. (1.85 m) is enough for a chain of five ornaments
- Two wooden spoons
- Two gummed picture hangers and stick pins for hanging on a wall. Or poster putty, for hanging on finished wood

4. Lace the ribbon through the holes, passing it behind each gingerbread man. Space the cutouts evenly on the ribbon.

5. Tie the ribbon ends in bows around wooden spoons. Apply poster putty to the back of each spoon, if hanging on finished wood. Or attach gummed picture hangers and hang from stick pins inserted into the wall.

1. In medium mixing bowl, combine cinnamon, cloves, and nutmeg. Add applesauce and glue. Mix well. Knead mixture in bowl or in hands until smooth and ingredients are well mixed.

2. Roll the dough flat to 1/4" (6 mm) thickness. (It may be easier to roll dough in batches, rather than all at once.) Cut out gingerbread men. Cut holes in the hands, using a drinking straw. Press beads and buttons gently in place, indenting dough slightly.

3. Place cutouts on wire racks; allow to dry at room temperature for 3 or more days. Glue the beads and buttons in place when completely dry. Add painted details.

Cookie Table

Divided into sections with simple streamers of wide ribbon, your dining room table is ready to be loaded up with packages of cookies. Just before leaving the party, each guest can easily walk around the table taking one package of cookies from each section.

Baking Tree

An adorably fitting centerpiece for your cookie table, this miniature Christmas tree is decorated with tiny baking utensils and cookie cutters, all tied up with tiny red bows. Look for these at specialty kitchen stores, toy stores, and antique shops.

Snack Buffet

Keeping it really casual, nonsweet appetizers and the all-important Christmas cookies are set out on the coffee table, an easy arm's reach away.

Bright Idea

Floor pillows provide extra seating and encourage a relaxing, casual atmosphere.

Coffee Bar

Conveniently located on the kitchen counter, a self-service coffee bar provides all the amenities of the local coffee shop. Assorted Christmas mugs, each waiting to be chosen, work double-duty as subtle conversation starters.

Chocolate Spoons

What You'll Need

- 4 oz. (113 g) high quality baking or dipping chocolate
- Vanilla chips
- Microwave oven
- $1/8$ to $1/4$ teaspoon (0.5 to 1 mL) oil flavoring of choice, optional
- 2-cup (500 mL) microwave-proof measuring cup
- 15 heavy-duty plastic spoons or decorative flatware spoons
- Baking sheet; wax paper

Quick and easy to make, but oh so delicious and impressive, these chocolate spoons turn an ordinary cup of coffee into a gourmet delight.

1. Break chocolate into small chunks, and place them in a measuring cup. Microwave at 50% for 2 to 3 minutes, or until chocolate is melted, stirring every minute for the first 2 minutes, then every 30 seconds. Stir in oil flavoring, if desired.

2. Dip a spoon into the melted chocolate, completely covering the bowl. Set the spoon on a wax-paper-lined baking sheet. Repeat with the remaining spoons. Allow the spoons to cool at room temperature.

3. Melt vanilla chips. Drizzle over the spoons.

Easy Creamy Fudge

Yield: 117 one-inch (2.5 cm) squares; enough to fill about 12 five-inch (12.5 cm) cookies cutters

- 1 lb. (450 g) powdered sugar (3¾ cups/925 mL)
- 2 eggs
- 12 oz. (340 g) semisweet chocolate, chopped
- 1 cup (250 mL) butter
- 1½ teaspoons (7 mL) vanilla extract

In large mixing bowl, combine sugar and eggs. Beat at low speed of electric mixer just until blended. Beat at medium speed until smooth. Set aside. Place chocolate in a medium mixing bowl. Melt butter in a saucepan over medium heat. Pour over chocolate. Whisk until smooth. Gradually whisk chocolate into sugar mixture. Mix well. Whisk in vanilla.

Pour into 9" × 13" (23 × 33 cm) pan and chill. Or make Fudge Favors, left.

Note: This recipe calls for raw eggs. If that concerns you, use pasteurized eggs. Frozen egg product is not a good substitute, however.

Per 1" (2.5 cm) square: Calories: 44
• Protein: <1 g. • Carbohydrate: 6 g. • Fat: 3 g.
• Cholesterol: 8 mg. • Sodium: 17 mg.
Exchanges: ½ fat, ⅓ other carbohydrate

Fudge Favors

As the hostess, you may decide to opt out of the cookie baking and make these party favors for your guests instead. Fudge-filled cookie cutters offer a fitting remembrance of a pleasurable time spent with friends, as well as sweet nibbling opportunities for days to come.

What You'll Need

- Recipe ingredients for Easy Creamy Fudge, right
- Large cookie cutters, one for each favor
- Baking candy decorations
- Wax paper
- Cookie sheets
- Clear cellophane; ribbon

1. Arrange cookie cutters on wax-paper-lined cookie sheets. Prepare the fudge recipe, following the directions at right. Spoon the fudge into the cookie cutters, filling almost to the top. Add baking candy decorations, as desired, while fudge is still warm. Chill.

2. Remove from wax paper; trim away any fudge that may have seeped under the cookie cutter. Wrap with cellophane and tie with ribbon. Keep refrigerated.

Hot Artichoke Ricotta Dip

Yield: 4 cups (1 L)

- 1 container (15 oz./425 g) whole-milk ricotta cheese
- 1 pkg. (10 oz./284 g) frozen artichoke hearts, thawed, drained, and chopped
- 1 cup (250 mL) shredded Parmesan cheese
- 1/4 cup (60 mL) finely chopped shallots
- 2 tablespoons (25 mL) lemon juice
- 1/2 teaspoon (2 mL) salt
- 1/2 teaspoon (2 mL) pepper
- 3 tablespoons (50 mL) dry unseasoned bread crumbs
- 2 tablespoons (25 mL) chopped pine nuts
- 1 tablespoon (15 mL) olive oil

Heat oven to 400°F/200°C. In a food processor or blender, process ricotta cheese until smooth and creamy. Combine in mixing bowl with artichokes, Parmesan, shallots, lemon juice, salt, and pepper. Spoon into 1-quart (1 L) casserole dish. In small bowl, combine remaining ingredients. Sprinkle mixture evenly over top. (Dip can be made to this point and refrigerated for several hours before baking.)

Bake dip, uncovered, for 20 to 25 minutes, or until browned on top and bubbly around edges. Serve with crackers, crusty French bread, or breadsticks.

Per 1/4 Cup (60 mL): Calories: 94 • Protein: 6 g. • Carbohydrate: 3 g.
• Fat: 7 g. • Cholesterol: 18 mg. • Sodium: 199 mg.
Exchanges: 3/4 high-fat meat, 1/8 starch, 1/4 vegetable

Sweet and Spicy Mixed Nuts

Yield: 2 cups (500 mL)

- 2 cups (500 mL) assorted nuts (pecans, blanched almonds, walnuts, hazelnuts, cashews, raw peanuts)
- 1/4 cup (59 mL) sugar
- 1 teaspoon (5 mL) kosher salt
- 1 teaspoon (5 mL) ground cinnamon
- 1/2 teaspoon (2 mL) ground ginger
- 1/4 teaspoon (1 mL) ground cumin
- 1/8 teaspoon (0.5 mL) ground cayenne
- Pinch ground cloves

Heat oven to 350°F/180°C. Spread nuts in single layer on baking sheet. Bake for 10 to 15 minutes, or until toasted, shaking pan once or twice.

Combine remaining ingredients in a small bowl. Place nuts in large skillet. Sprinkle spice mixture over top. Cook nuts over medium heat for 8 to 10 minutes, or until sugar melts and nuts are coated, stirring occasionally.

Spread nuts on lightly oiled baking sheet to cool. Store in airtight container in cool place.

Note: You will have better results if you make several single batches, than if you try to fit a double batch in one skillet.

Per 1/4 Cup (60 mL): Calories: 217 • Protein: 4 g. • Carbohydrate: 12 g. • Fat: 18 g.
• Cholesterol: 0 mg. • Sodium: 186 mg.
Exchanges: 1/2 high-fat meat, 2 3/4 fat, 3/4 other carbohydrate

Herb and Cheese Biscuit Sandwiches

Yield: 24 biscuits

- 2 cups (500 mL) all-purpose flour
- 1 tablespoon (15 mL) baking powder
- 1/2 teaspoon (2 mL) salt
- 1/4 cup (60 mL) butter, chilled and chopped
- 1/3 cup (75 mL) herbed cream cheese, chilled
- 3/4 cup (175 mL) whole milk

In large mixing bowl, combine flour, baking powder, and salt. Cut in butter and cream cheese until mixture resembles coarse crumbs. Stir milk in with fork until mixture can be shaped into a ball.

Place dough on lightly floured surface. Roll into a 16" × 10" (40.5 × 25.5 cm) rectangle. Fold in short sides so they meet in the middle. Fold again in half from left to right. Roll out to a 12" × 8" (30.5 × 20.5 cm) rectangle, 1/2" (1.3 cm) thick. Cut dough into 2" (5 cm) rounds or squares. If cutting rounds, reroll and cut out scraps as before.

Arrange rounds or squares on baking sheet. Chill for 20 minutes. Heat oven to 425°F/220°C. Bake for 13 to 15 minutes, or until golden. Cool biscuits on cooling racks. Use biscuits to make small sandwiches. Below are some suggestions, but you can use any fillings you like.

Sandwich-filling suggestions: shaved meats (ham, roast beef, smoked turkey, Italian deli meats), cheeses (Swiss, Cheddar, goat cheese, Havarti, Muenster), garnishes (sliced cornichon pickles, pickled asparagus spears, watercress), and condiments (mayonnaise, mustard, horseradish, dressing).

Per Biscuit: Calories: 73 • Protein: 2 g. • Carbohydrate: 9 g. • Fat: 3 g. • Cholesterol: 10 mg. • Sodium: 145 mg.
Exchanges: 1/2 starch, 3/4 fat

Raspberry Stars

Yield: 48 cookies

- 1 cup (250 mL) butter, softened
- $1/2$ cup plus 2 tablespoons (150 mL) sugar
- $2 1/4$ cups (550 mL) all-purpose flour
- Pinch salt
- 1 cup (250 mL) seedless raspberry jam

Icing:
- 1 cup (250 mL) powdered sugar
- 2 teaspoons (10 mL) almond extract
- 2 to 3 teaspoons (10 to 15 mL) water

Heat oven to 350°F/180°C. In medium mixing bowl, cream together butter and sugar. Stir in flour and salt. Roll dough into 1" (2.5 cm) balls. Place on cookie sheets 2" (5 cm) apart. Press balls to $3/8$" (1 cm) thickness. Indent cookies with thumb, back of spoon, or thimble.

Spoon jam into sealable plastic bag. Seal bag. Snip hole in one corner of bag. Squeeze jam into indents in cookies. Bake for 10 to 12 minutes, or until golden brown around edges. Let cookies sit on cookie sheet 2 minutes before removing to cooling rack.

Meanwhile, combine icing ingredients. Spoon icing into second sealable plastic bag. Seal bag. Snip very small hole in corner of bag. Squeeze icing onto cooled cookies in shape of star.

Per Cookie: Calories: 93 • Protein: 1 g. • Carbohydrate: 14 g. • Fat: 4 g. • Cholesterol: 10 mg. • Sodium: 42 mg. Exchanges: $1/4$ starch, $3/4$ fat, $3/4$ other carbohydrate

Sugar Plums

Yield: 36 sugar plums

- $3/4$ cup (175 mL) granulated sugar
- $1/2$ cup (125 mL) finely chopped dried apricots
- $1/2$ cup (125 mL) finely chopped pitted dates or dried figs
- 2 eggs, beaten
- 1 cup (250 mL) finely chopped blanched almonds, toasted*
- 1 teaspoon (5 mL) grated orange peel
- 1 teaspoon (5 mL) vanilla extract
- $1/2$ teaspoon (2 mL) ground cinnamon
- $1/4$ teaspoon (1 mL) ground allspice
- $1/4$ teaspoon (1 mL) ground nutmeg
- Pinch salt
- Granulated and/or powdered sugar

In medium saucepan, combine $3/4$ cup (175 mL) granulated sugar, the apricots, dates, and eggs. Cook over medium-low heat for 6 to 8 minutes, or until mixture pulls away from sides of pan, stirring constantly.

Remove from heat. Stir in almonds, orange peel, vanilla, cinnamon, allspice, nutmeg, and salt. Let stand for 30 minutes, or until cool enough to handle. Mixture will be sticky. Use 2 tableware teaspoons to scoop up mixture and roughly shape it into 1" (2.5 cm) balls. Finish shaping balls by rolling them in granulated or powdered sugar. To store, refrigerate sugar plums in airtight container between sheets of wax paper.

Toast almonds before chopping. To toast almonds, spread them on a baking sheet. Bake in 400°F/200°C oven for 10 minutes, shaking pan once.

Tip: Sugar plums will absorb powdered sugar over time. Roll them again in powdered sugar just before serving.

Per Sugar Plum: Calories: 64 • Protein: 1 g. • Carbohydrate: 10 g. • Fat: 2 g. • Cholesterol: 12 mg. • Sodium: 8 mg. Exchanges: $1/8$ high-fat meat, $1/3$ fruit, $1/4$ fat, $1/3$ other carbohydrate

Chocolate-Dipped Hazelnut Biscotti

Yield: 42 biscotti

- 1 cup (250 mL) slivered almonds
- 1 1/2 cups (375 mL) sugar
- 1/2 cup (125 mL) unsalted butter, softened
- 1 tablespoon (25 mL) hazelnut liqueur
- 3 eggs
- 3 3/4 cups (925 mL) all-purpose flour
- 2 teaspoons (10 mL) baking powder
- Pinch salt
- 1 cup (250 mL) milk chocolate chips
- 2 teaspoons (10 mL) vegetable shortening
- 1/2 cup (125 mL) finely chopped hazelnuts

Heat oven to 350°F/180°C. Lightly grease cookie sheets. Set aside. Place almonds in 8-inch (2 L) square baking pan. Bake for 10 to 12 minutes, or until light golden brown, stirring occasionally. Coarsely chop almonds. Set aside.

In large mixing bowl, combine sugar, butter, and liqueur. Beat at medium speed of electric mixer until light and fluffy. Add eggs, one at a time, beating after each addition. Add flour, baking powder, and salt. Beat at low speed until soft dough forms. Stir in almonds.

Divide dough into quarters. On lightly floured surface, shape each quarter into 2" (5 cm) wide log. Place logs 2" (5 cm) apart on prepared cookie sheet. Bake for 30 to 35 minutes, or until golden brown.

Immediately cut hot logs diagonally into 3/4" (2 cm) slices. Place slices 1" (2.5 cm) apart on prepared cookie sheets. Bake for additional 10 to 15 minutes, or until dry and golden brown. Cool completely.

In 1-quart (1 L) saucepan, combine chocolate chips and shortening. Melt over low heat, stirring constantly. Remove from heat. Dip one end of each cookie diagonally into melted chocolate. Sprinkle hazelnuts evenly over dipped ends. Let dry completely before storing in airtight container.

Per Biscotti: Calories: 147 • Protein: 2 g. • Carbohydrate: 19 g. • Fat: 7 g. • Cholesterol: 21 mg. • Sodium: 33 mg.
Exchanges: 3/4 starch, 1 1/4 fat, 1/2 other carbohydrate

New Year's Eve Bash

Hopes for the year ahead mingle with fond memories of days past to make your New Year's Eve celebration a joyous lighthearted affair. Star-studded and glitzy, the festivities are a perfect send-off with a bright new beginning.

Menu

Antipasto Platter

Puff Pastry Braids

Cheesy Salmon Pinwheels

Wonton Cups with Holiday Chicken Salad

Asian Beef Salad in Cucumber Cups

Sherry Buttercream Cake

Pull out all the stops to make this party a fun-filled flashy production, starring a cast of dear friends, both new and old. Illuminate the night with twinkling white lights, glimmering candles, and the glint of colorful metallic accents throughout your home. Enlist the reflective power of chrome or silver serving pieces, mixed with the light-refracting qualities of cut glass and crystal. To emphasize the timely count-down, prominently display alarm clocks set to simultaneously ring in the new year. Stock the bar with a variety of refreshments, including plenty of nonalcoholic choices. For help-yourself dining throughout the evening, set out a lavish buffet of finger foods. Plan a few rousing activities to involve all of your guests in the merrymaking and seemingly shorten the wait for that all-important midnight hour.

Starry Invitations

Let's ring in the
New year with
"alarming" fun!

Festivities will start around 8:00 pm and
run until the champagne is gone, well
after midnight.

R.S.V.P. TO DIANE BY THE 25TH

What You'll Need

- Card stock; 8½" x 11" (21.8 x 28 cm)
- Translucent vellum
- Computer (optional)
- Rubber star stamps; stamp pads
- Large metallic star stickers

1. Mark light pencil lines in both directions through the center of a sheet of card stock. Fold the long outer edges to the center; crease and unfold. Fold the short edges to the center; crease and unfold. Erase the pencil lines.

2. Trim away the corners as shown, cutting a straight edge on the foldline and rounding the remaining edge on each flap.

3. Print the party information on the vellum, using a computer or by hand. Cut it into a rectangle, slightly smaller than the inside rectangle of the invitation.

4. Stamp stars randomly over both sides of the invitation, allowing room for the address. With vellum in center, fold in the flaps consecutively, covering the straight edges. Tuck in the last square corner. Seal with a star sticker.

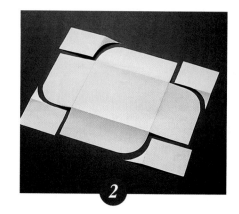

What You'll Need

- Two strings of white outdoor lights with white cords
- Two or three different metallic garlands
- Two or three different metallic ribbons
- Floral paddle wire; eye screws
- Curly willow branches, painted silver
- Large aluminum pail
- Sand

Sparkling Entry

Dress up your doorstep with a spectacular lighted garland and a spray of silver curly willow branches.

1. Loosely twist one light string with the metallic garlands and the ribbons. Secure the garland to the door frame, using floral wire and eye screws. Or attach the garland to a railing.

2. Form the remaining ribbon into bows, and secure them to the garland at the points of attachment.

3. Fill the pail with sand and insert the curly willow branches. Wind the remaining lights around the branches. Embellish the pail with a silver bow.

Candlelit Mantel

Decorate your mantel or a side table with a glittering star garland, sheer silver ribbons, and candles. Add small silver balls, crystals, or mirrors to reflect and amplify the candlelight.

Tinsel Ball Bowl

Accent an end table or powder room vanity with a sparkling bowl. Fill clear glass ball ornaments with shredded or curled tinsel. Place the battery pack for a string of battery-operated lights in the center of a clear glass bowl. Arrange the ornaments and lights in the bowl, hiding the battery pack.

Celestial Streamers

Hang bright crepe paper and metallic streamers from the ceiling above the buffet table or in other areas less traveled. To avoid marring your ceiling, attach each streamer using a dot of removable poster putty. Hang twinkling metallic stars at different heights among the streamers.

Timely Centerpiece

Keep your guests ever aware of the time with a whimsical buffet table accent that includes strategically placed alarm clocks. Of course, you must set the clocks to go off at midnight, signalling the new year. Complete the arrangement with mirrors, sprinkled confetti, candles, and ribbon.

Iced Champagne Bucket

What You'll Need

- Clear acrylic ice bucket
- Empty plastic or glass jar with slightly larger diameter than champagne bottle
- Rocks
- Water
- Food coloring (optional)

1. Place the jar in the center of the ice bucket. Insert rocks for weight. Pour water into the ice bucket almost to the top of the jar. Add food coloring, if desired. Freeze the water.

2. Remove the rocks. Pour warm water into jar to release it from the ice. Remove the jar. Place champagne bottle in the well of the ice before serving.

Bright Idea

Have a large white dinner napkin handy when pouring the champagne, to dry off the outside of the bottle and catch any drips.

Painted Glassware

Give inexpensive wine glasses a touch of elegance with Krylon® Metallic Leafing Pens and a little ribbon. Paint simple star shapes on the outer surface of the glasses. Tie bows at the tops of the stems with narrow sheer ribbon.

Napkins and Coasters

Wrap paper napkins around forks and seal them with a star sticker. Make quick and easy coasters, using metallic cardboard stars, available at paper product stores. Keep them all easily accessible in silver star-shaped baskets at the buffet table.

Fortune Cake

Bake a special cake and hide secret fortunes between the layers. After serving the cake, have each guest pull on the ribbon to discover what the new year might have in store.

What You'll Need

- Ingredients for making Sherry Buttercream Cake, as listed on page 117
- Paper
- Computer (optional)
- Clear self-adhesive laminating plastic
- Hole punch
- Curling ribbon

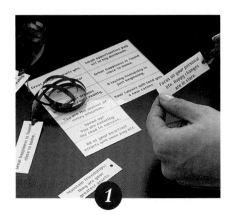

1. Print out fortunes in two evenly spaced columns on a sheet of paper. Plan for each fortune to be slightly narrower than a wedge of the cake. Laminate the paper on both sides, using clear self-adhesive plastic. Cut the fortunes apart. Punch a hole near one end of each fortune. Tie a ribbon through each hole.

2. Prepare the cake layers and frosting, as on page 117. Arrange the fortunes between the cake layers so that when the cake is cut, each serving will have a fortune. Allow the ribbon ends to extend out beyond the frosting where they can be easily grasped.

Zero Hour

Hand out noise makers, hats, and horns from a large basket embellished with metallic curling ribbon. Make sure you have enough for everyone!

Confetti Balloons

Pour confetti into large balloons using a funnel. Then fill the balloons with helium and tie them in bunches to weights. Pass out a few push pins for popping the balloons when the alarm clocks go off.

Antipasto Platter

The antipasto platter can easily be the most impressive thing on the buffet table—and the most simple to prepare. This is a case where presentation is everything, because all the components for the platter are purchased ready-made. All you have to do is buy an assortment of cured Italian meats, pickled or cured vegetables, good cheeses, and crusty Italian bread.

Cured Meats: Assorted Italian meats, or *salumi*, are key elements to the antipasto platter. Purchase them at an Italian market or the deli section of the supermarket. Prosciutto, coppacola, sopresatta, and mortadella are some of the Italian meats you may see. If they seem unfamiliar, ask to taste before you buy. If you can't find Italian specialty meats, just buy the best cured meats you can. High-quality ham, salami, seasoned turkey breast, and smoked roast beef work fine.

Pickled/Cured Vegetables: Pickled or marinated vegetables, like pepperoncini peppers, asparagus, artichoke hearts, roasted red peppers, mushrooms, and onions, are available in jars in most supermarkets. In larger stores, you can find assorted cured olives and pickled vegetable blends at the deli counter. Use these items to add color and spice to the antipasto platter.

Cheeses: Cheeses like fresh mozzarella, Parmesan, and Gorgonzola (a kind of blue cheese) are essential to the antipasto platter. Get the best you can find. Fresh mozzarella can be cubed or sliced, then dipped in olive oil and rolled in chopped fresh basil. Look for a high-quality Parmesan, like Parmigiano-Reggiano. Then break it into small chunks for the platter.

Bread: Finally, a basket filled with sliced Italian bread is the only accompaniment to the antipasto platter. Look for one with a firm texture and chewy crust. If you like, you could toast slices, then rub them with garlic and drizzle with olive oil to make bruschetta.

Assembling the Platter: Figuring out the best way to display all these good things is the only hard part. Just remember to keep it simple and don't overcrowd. Better to do more than one platter, than to cram it all on one. Put oily or marinated items in small bowls to either set on the platter or next to it. Roll or fold cured meats, then arrange them overlapping each other. Overlap slices of fresh mozzarella and pieces of roasted red pepper for contrasting colors. Arrange vegetables in little piles next to the meats. Finally, scatter chunks of Parmesan and Gorgonzola around the platter to fill in gaps.

Puff Pastry Braids

Yield: 20 braids

- 1 box (17.3 oz./490 g) frozen puff pastry sheets, thawed
- 5 oz. (140 g) deli-sliced ham

Heat oven to 400°F/200°C. Lay puff pastry sheets on work surface. Press out creases. Cut each sheet crosswise into 20 strips, about ⅜" (1 cm) thick. Cut ham into ½" (1.3 cm) strips.

Press the end of one strip of ham between the ends of two strips of puff pastry. Braid the three strips together. (Depending on the length of the ham strips, you may need to add a second strip of ham halfway through braiding.) Press ends together to seal. Lay braid on baking sheet. Repeat with remaining puff pastry and ham strips.

Bake braids for 12 to 14 minutes, or until pastry is golden. Carefully, transfer braids to cooling rack. (They will firm up as they cool.) Store in airtight container.

Notes: These braids are best if eaten the same day they are made.

For looks, sprinkle braids with Italian seasoning, poppy seeds, or kosher salt before baking.

Per Braid: Calories: 147 • Protein: 3 g. • Carbohydrate: 11 g. • Fat: 10 g.
• Cholesterol: 4 mg. • Sodium: 152 mg.
Exchanges: ¾ starch, ¼ lean meat, 1½ fat

Cheesy Salmon Pinwheels

Yield: 18 pinwheels

- 1 container (8 oz./227 g) vegetable-flavored cream cheese
- 3 tablespoons (50 mL) grated Parmesan cheese
- 2 tablespoons (25 mL) minced fresh chives
- 1 teaspoon (5 mL) milk or cream
- ¼ teaspoon (1 mL) freshly ground pepper
- 4 flour tortillas (10"/25.5 cm diameter)
- 9 oz. (250 g) smoked salmon (lox-style salmon)

In a small mixing bowl, combine cheeses, chives, milk, and pepper. Spread mixture evenly on tortillas. Arrange salmon slices evenly over cheese mixture. Roll up tortillas to enclose fillings. Wrap in plastic wrap, and chill at least 1 hour.

Trim ends off tortilla rolls. Cut each roll into nine pinwheels, about ½" (1.3 cm) thick.

Alternatives: Substitute deli-sliced ham, roast beef or turkey for salmon. If you can find them, substitute colored or herbed tortillas for flour tortillas.

Substitute deli-sliced ham for the tortillas and roasted red, green, or yellow peppers for the salmon. Secure sliced pinwheels with wooden picks.

Per 2 Pinwheels: Calories: 105 • Protein: 5 g. • Carbohydrate: 8 g. • Fat: 6 g.
• Cholesterol: 16 mg. • Sodium: 402 mg.
Exchanges: ½ starch, ½ lean meat, ¾ fat

Wonton Cups with Holiday Chicken Salad

Yield: 24 wonton cups

- 24 wonton wrappers
- 1 boneless, skinless chicken breast half (4 oz./114 g), cooked
- $1/4$ cup (60 mL) chopped fresh or frozen cranberries
- 2 tablespoons (25 mL) chopped green onions
- 1 tablespoon (15 mL) chopped fresh cilantro or flat-leaf parsley
- 2 teaspoons (10 mL) chopped crystallized ginger
- 1 teaspoon (5 mL) grated orange peel
- $1/4$ teaspoon (1 mL) salt
- $1/4$ cup (60 mL) mayonnaise
- 24 whole roasted cashews

Heat oven to 350°F/180°C. Trim wonton wrappers to make 3" (7.5 cm) squares. Spray 24-cup mini-muffin tin with nonstick vegetable cooking spray. Press 1 wrapper into each cup. Lightly spray wrappers with cooking spray. Bake for 6 to 8 minutes, or until lightly browned. Cool cups on wire rack. (Store up to one week in airtight container.)

For salad, finely chop chicken ($1/4$"/6 mm cubes). Combine with remaining ingredients, except mayonnaise and cashews. Add mayonnaise and stir to coat. Chill for at least 1 hour. Fill wonton cups just before serving. Garnish each with a cashew.

Note: Eggroll skins can also be trimmed into 3" (7.5 cm) squares. You'll need 6 eggroll skins to make 24 cups.

Per 3-Piece Serving: Calories: 148 • Protein: 6 g. • Carbohydrate: 13 g. • Fat: 8 g.
• Cholesterol: 14 mg. • Sodium: 225 mg.
Exchanges: $1/2$ lean meat, $3/4$ starch, $1 1/4$ fat, $1/8$ other carbohydrate

Asian Beef Salad in Cucumber Cups

In a sealable plastic bag, combine marinade ingredients. Add steak. Seal bag and turn to coat steak. Refrigerate for one hour, turning bag occasionally. Heat oil in skillet over medium heat. Drain and discard marinade from steak. Cook steak in skillet for 4 to 6 minutes per side, or until desired doneness. Set steak aside until cool enough to handle.

Cut steak into small strips, about 2" × $1/4$" (5 cm × 6 mm). Combine steak in medium mixing bowl with cilantro, hoisin sauce, vinegar, and chile. Cover and chill until ready to fill cups.

Trim ends from cucumbers. Cut cucumbers into 1" (2.5 cm) sections. Hollow out each section with a melon baller to make cups, leaving bottom of cups intact. Just before serving, spoon steak mixture evenly into cups. Sprinkle lightly with sesame seeds.

Notes: The beef salad and cups can be prepared ahead separately. Don't fill cups until just before serving to preserve freshness of cucumbers.

For more decorative cups, cut wedges out of top edge with paring knife.

Per 2-Piece Serving: Calories: 65 • Protein: 5 g. • Carbohydrate: 3 g. • Fat: 3 g.
• Cholesterol: 15 mg. • Sodium: 214 mg.
Exchanges: $2/3$ lean meat, $2/3$ vegetable, $1/3$ fat

Yield: 18 cucumber cups

Marinade:
- $1/2$ cup (125 mL) soy sauce
- $1/4$ cup (60 mL) seasoned rice vinegar
- 2 tablespoons (25 mL) dried minced onions
- 2 tablespoons (25 mL) sugar
- 2 teaspoons (10 mL) ground ginger
- 1 tablespoon (15 mL) minced garlic

- 1 lb. (450 g) sirloin steak, 1" (2.5 cm) thick

- 1 tablespoon (15 mL) sesame oil
- $1/3$ cup (75 mL) chopped fresh cilantro
- 2 tablespoons (25 mL) hoisin sauce
- 2 tablespoons (25 mL) seasoned rice vinegar
- 2 teaspoons (10 mL) finely chopped seeded red chile
- 4 English cucumbers, 10" (25.5 cm) long
- Sesame seeds

Sherry Buttercream Cake

Yield: 16 servings

Cake:
- 1 box (1 lb. 2.25 oz./517 g) yellow cake mix
- 1 box (3 oz./85 g) cook-and-serve vanilla pudding mix
- 4 eggs
- 3/4 cup (175 mL) dry sherry
- 3/4 cup (175 mL) vegetable oil

Sherry Buttercream:
- 1 1/2 cups (375 mL) sugar
- 3/4 cup (175 mL) water
- 1/4 teaspoon (1 mL) cream of tartar
- 3 large eggs
- 1 lb. (450 g) (4 sticks) butter, room temperature
- 2 tablespoons (25 mL) dry sherry

Heat oven to 350°F/180°. Spray two 8" (20.5 cm) round cake pans with nonstick vegetable cooking spray. Line each with parchment paper circle. Spray paper with cooking spray. Set aside.

In a large mixing bowl, combine cake ingredients. Beat at low speed of electric mixer just until blended. Beat at medium speed for 2 minutes. Pour batter evenly into prepared pans. Bake for 25 to 30 minutes, or until wooden pick inserted in center comes out clean. Run knife around edge of pans to loosen cakes. Turn onto wire racks. Remove paper and cool completely.

With serrated bread knife, level tops of cakes. Cut cakes in half horizontally. Wrap four layers with plastic wrap. Freeze.

For buttercream, combine sugar, water, and cream of tartar in small saucepan. Bring to a boil over medium heat, stirring until sugar is dissolved. Let boil, uncovered, for 20 to 25 minutes, or until mixture reaches soft-ball stage (238°F/113°C) on candy thermometer.

While sugar syrup boils, beat eggs in top of double boiler off heat at medium speed of electric mixer for 5 to 7 minutes, or until thick and pale. Bring 1" (2.5 cm) of water to a simmer in bottom of double boiler. When syrup reaches

soft-ball stage, begin beating eggs at medium speed. While beating, add syrup to eggs in slow, steady drizzle. After syrup is added, place eggs over simmering water. Cook for 3 to 5 minutes, or until mixture reads 160°F/70°C on instant-read thermometer, beating at low speed.

Remove from heat and pour egg mixture into large mixing bowl. Beat at medium speed for 15 to 20 minutes, or until mixture cools to 80°F/27°C. Beat in butter 1 tablespoon (15 mL) at a time, making sure each tablespoon is incorporated before adding the next. When all the butter is in, beat in sherry.

Place one frozen layer of cake on serving plate. Spread a layer of buttercream on top. Repeat with next two layers. Top with remaining layer. Spread thin layer of buttercream over entire cake. Spoon some buttercream into pastry bag fitted with star tip. Pipe small stars over sides and top of cake. Chill cake until serving time.

Note: Buttercream can be made ahead and chilled. Let it come to room temperature and beat at medium speed of electric mixer before frosting cake.

Per Serving: Calories: 560 • Protein: 5 g. • Carbohydrate: 52 g. • Fat: 39 g. • Cholesterol: 155 mg. • Sodium: 508 mg.
Exchanges: 1 1/2 starch, 7 1/2 fat, 2 other carbohydrate

Holiday Brunch

A festive late morning meal, perhaps served to out-of-town guests, is a soul-warming start for a special day. A formal table setting and lavish holiday decor create a grand aura for even the simplest gathering.

Menu

Classic Scones and Blue Cheese Butter

Citrus with Raspberry Coulis

Cordon Bleu Roulade with Red Wine Sauce

Hearty Hazelnut Wild Rice

Mixed Greens Salad

Double Berry Mousse

Though brunch may carry an ordinary reputation, surprise your guests with a tantalizing menu that will really wake up their taste buds and energize them for a fun-packed day. With your finest dinnerware at an elegantly set table, treat your special guests to a formal sit-down brunch, giving each delicious course the time and attention it deserves. Incorporate fresh fruit into the meal and carry the fruit theme in your decorations to breathe cheery life into a wintry day. With curtains drawn back to welcome the view, take advantage of morning sunlight, even if it happens to be reflecting off a snow-covered landscape.

Holly Invitations

Extend your invitation on a simple holly cutout enclosed with a Christmas letter. Hand-write the message and line the edges of the leaf in gold ink.

Twig Window Wreaths

What You'll Need

- Small twig wreaths, one for each window
- Greens, such as boxwood, holly, or seeded eucalyptus
- Small colorful artificial fruits, such as kumquats, cherries, grapes, pears, and apples
- Wired ribbon
- Hot glue gun

Chandelier Accent

Embellish your chandelier with some of the same elements used in the wreaths,
keeping the elements well away from the lightbulbs. Secure greens and berry stems
to the chandelier arms, using floral wire. Top it off with a flourish of ribbon.

1. Cut small branches of two or three
different greens, and arrange around
the twig wreath. Secure the ends with
hot glue.

2. Arrange colorful artificial fruits
around the center ring of the wreath.
Secure them in place with hot glue.

3. Insert a length of ribbon through
the center of the wreath for hanging in
the window. Tie the ends in a bow.
Hang the wreath from the top of the
window frame on casement windows
or from the window lock on double-
hung windows.

Snowy Fruit Centerpiece

Create a tiered centerpiece with sugared fruits and berries, laced with fresh sprigs of greenery. Top off the creation with a light sprinkling of powdered sugar.

What You'll Need

- Large glass plate
- Two footed glass plates with smaller diameters
- Floral putty
- Fresh colorful fruits
- Fresh greens
- Egg white; soft paintbrush
- Sugar
- Confectioner's sugar and a sifter

1. Stack the three glass serving pieces. Secure each with a small amount of floral putty. Arrange the greens sparingly on each layer.

2. Brush fruits and berries on one side with egg white; dip in sugar, and allow to dry. Arrange the larger pieces evenly on all three plate layers; fill in with smaller pieces.

3. Sprinkle confectioner's sugar lightly over the arrangement, using a sifter.

Stenciled Placemats

Turn plain purchased placemats into something special by stenciling holly sprigs around the outer edges.

What You'll Need

- Cream-colored fabric placemats
- Holly stencil
- Repositionable spray adhesive
- Sponge pouncers
- Acrylic fabric paints in green and red
- Paper plate; paper towels

1. Wash and dry the placemats to remove any finishes that might prohibit the paint from adhering to the fibers. Spray the back of the stencil plates with repositionable spray adhesive; wait a few minutes before using the stencil.

2. Position the first stencil plate in one corner of the placemat; press all around to secure it to the fabric. If there is only one plate for the stencil, mask off any areas that should not be painted with the first color.

3. Pour a small amount of the paint onto a paper plate. Dip the pouncer in the paint; blot excess on a paper towel. Pounce over the stencil, shading the outer rim of each design area darker than the center.

4. Remove the stencil plate and repeat the process with each plate of the stencil. Or remask the stencil if there is only one plate, and repeat the process with each color. Allow the paint to dry. Heat-set the design, following the manufacturer's directions.

Ribbon-Tied Napkins

Tie cloth napkins with gold wired ribbon for an elegant touch. Tuck a couple of silk holly sprigs into the bow.

Gold Chargers

Stack the plates for each course of the brunch on a gold charger. After seating, remove the plates from the charger and serve the courses one plate at a time.

Miniature Fruit Basket Favors

Mark each place setting with a personalized miniature fruit basket ornament. The ornament will always carry with it warm memories of your special brunch.

What You'll Need

- Miniature handled basket, one for each place setting
- Hot glue gun
- Gold angel hair
- Artificial or preserved greens
- Artificial berries and miniature fruits
- Small craft bird
- Narrow gold ribbon
- Place cards
- Hole punch

1. Secure a "nest" of gold angel hair to the basket bottom, using hot glue.

2. Insert several sprigs of artificial or preserved greens. Fill spaces between the greens with berries and miniature fruits. Secure with hot glue.

3. Secure the bird to the edge of the basket with hot glue. Punch a small hole at one corner of the place card. Insert ribbon through the hole and tie a bow onto the basket handle.

recipes

Blue Cheese Butter

Yield: 1 cup (250 mL)

- 1/2 cup (125 mL) butter, softened
- 4 oz. (114 g) blue cheese, crumbled

Blend butter and cheese together with fork until uniform consistency. Serve at room temperature.

Per 1 Tablespoon (15 mL): Calories: 76 • Protein: 2 g. • Carbohydrate: <1 g. • Fat: 8 g. • Cholesterol: 21 mg. • Sodium: 157 mg. Exchanges: 1/4 high-fat meat, 1 fat

Classic Scones

Yield: 24 scones

- 3 cups (750 mL) all-purpose flour
- 1 tablespoon (15 mL) baking powder
- 1 tablespoon (15 mL) sugar
- 1/2 teaspoon (2 mL) salt
- 6 tablespoons (85 mL) butter, chilled and cubed
- 3 eggs
- 2/3 cup (150 mL) whole milk

Heat oven to 425°F/220°C. In large mixing bowl, combine flour, baking powder, sugar, and salt. Cut in butter until mixture resembles coarse crumbs. Add eggs and milk. Stir until well combined.

Turn dough onto lightly floured surface. Knead 2 to 3 minutes, or until smooth. Roll dough to 16" × 6" (40.5 × 15 cm) rectangle, 3/4" (2 cm) thick. Cut rectangle in half lengthwise, then crosswise 12 small rectangles. Cut each small rectangle into two triangles. Place on baking sheet.

Bake for 12 to 15 minutes, or until scones are golden and crusty. Serve warm with Blue Cheese Butter (page 125), jam, or orange marmalade.

Note: Scones are best fresh from the oven, but they may be baked ahead and reheated before serving. They will just lose a little of their crustiness.

Per Scone: Calories: 99 • Protein: 3 g. • Carbohydrate: 13 g. • Fat: 4 g.
• Cholesterol: 35 mg. • Sodium: 150 mg.
Exchanges: 1 starch, 1/2 fat

Citrus with Raspberry Coulis

In medium saucepan, combine berries, sugar, orange juice, and peel. Bring to a simmer over medium heat. Simmer for 10 minutes, stirring to break up berries. Strain mixture through fine-mesh sieve to remove seeds. Return to clean saucepan.

Return to simmer over medium heat. Simmer for 10 minutes, or until slightly thickened. Stir in liqueur. Cool coulis to room temperature before serving.

Use a knife to cut white membrane away from outside of peeled grapefruit and oranges. Cut between membranes to release sections.

Spoon a pool of coulis on each serving plate. Fan grapefruit and orange sections on pools. Drizzle with additional coulis.

Note: Coulis can be made ahead and chilled. Cover it with plastic wrap touching its surface to prevent a skin from forming.

Yield: 8 servings

- 2 pkgs. (12 oz./340 g each) frozen raspberries
- 1 cup (250 mL) sugar
- 1 cup (250 mL) orange juice
- 1 tablespoon (15 mL) grated orange peel
- 1 tablespoon (15 mL) orange-flavored liqueur (optional)
- 4 grapefruit, peeled
- 4 oranges, peeled

Per Serving: Calories: 231 • Protein: 2 g. • Carbohydrate: 59 g. • Fat: 1 g.
• Cholesterol: 0 mg. • Sodium: 1 mg.
Exchanges: 2 1/4 fruit, 1 2/3 other carbohydrate

Cordon Bleu Roulade

Yield: 8 servings

- 4 whole (unsplit) chicken breasts (1 lb./450 g each), boneless, skinless
- Four pieces cheesecloth, single layer (16" x 12"/40.5 x 30.5 cm)
- 1 to 2 tablespoons (15 to 25 mL) olive oil
- 2 cups (500 mL) shredded Gruyere or Swiss cheese
- 16 to 20 large leaves fresh spinach
- 8 oz. (227 g) deli-sliced smoked ham

Heat oven to 350°F/180°C. Lay chicken breasts out flat. Trim away any fat and discard. Trim off thick portions of breast. Use thick portions to fit between breast halves to level them and fill gaps.

Soak cheesecloth in olive oil. Squeeze out cheesecloth and spread pieces on work surface. Sprinkle open chicken breasts evenly with cheese. Layer with a single layer of spinach leaves, then top with ham. Tightly roll up breasts from side to side, tucking in ends as you roll. Wrap rolled breasts tightly in prepared cheesecloth pieces. (Chicken breasts may be prepared to this point and refrigerated several hours before roasting.)

Arrange rolled chicken breasts seam side down on rack in roasting pan. Roast for 45 minutes. Remove from oven and remove cheesecloth. Increase oven temperature to 450°F/230°C. Return breasts to oven. Roast for 15 to 20 minutes longer, until internal temperature in breasts is 155°F/68°C. Remove from oven and cover with foil. Let stand 10 minutes before slicing. Slice rolled breasts crosswise. Serve with Red Wine Sauce, below.

Per Serving: Calories: 410 • Protein: 67 g. • Carbohydrate: 1 g. • Fat: 14 g. • Cholesterol: 176 mg. • Sodium: 654 mg.
Exchanges: 9^1/$_2$ very lean meat, 1^3/$_4$ fat

Red Wine Sauce

Yield: 1^3/$_4$ cups (425 mL)

- 1 tablespoon (15 mL) olive oil
- ^{1}/$_2$ cup (125 mL) finely chopped shallots
- 2 tablespoons (25 mL) tomato paste
- 2 teaspoons (10 mL) minced garlic
- 1 cup (250 mL) dry red wine
- 1^1/$_2$ cups (375 mL) beef broth
- 1 tablespoon (15 mL) cornstarch dissolved in 1 tablespoon (15 mL) water
- ^{1}/$_2$ teaspoon (2 mL) salt
- ^{1}/$_4$ teaspoon (1 mL) pepper
- 1 tablespoon (15 mL) butter (optional)

Heat oil in medium saucepan over medium heat. Add shallots and sauté for 3 to 4 minutes, until tender. Add tomato paste and garlic. Sauté for 2 minutes. Add wine, stirring to loosen any browned bits from bottom of pan. Let boil for 5 to 7 minutes, or until wine is reduced by half. Add broth and bring to a simmer. Whisk in cornstarch mixture. Cook for 1 to 2 minutes, or until thickened. Strain sauce through fine-mesh sieve. Stir in salt, pepper, and butter.

Note: Sauce may be made in advance, refrigerated, and reheated.

Per ^{1}/$_4$ Cup (60 mL): Calories: 42 • Protein: 1 g. • Carbohydrate: 5 g. • Fat: 2 g.
• Cholesterol: 1 mg. • Sodium: 381 mg.
Exchanges: ^{1}/$_2$ fat, ^{1}/$_3$ other carbohydrate

Mixed Greens Salad with Goat Cheese Croutons

In small bowl, combine crumbs and nuts. Brush goat cheese slices all over with oil. Dredge cheese slices in crumb mixture to coat. Arrange on baking sheet. Cover croutons with plastic wrap and refrigerate until ready to serve.

For salad, toss greens with vinaigrette to coat. Arrange dressed greens on salad plates. Meanwhile, broil croutons 4" (10 cm) from heat for 2 to 3 minutes, or until golden on top. Arrange 2 or 3 croutons on each salad. Sprinkle salads evenly with raspberries. Top salads with freshly cracked pepper. Serve immediately.

Per Serving: Calories: 303 • Protein: 10 g. • Carbohydrate: 14 g.
• Fat: 23 g. • Cholesterol: 30 mg. • Sodium: 471 mg.
Exchanges: 1 high-fat meat, 1/4 starch, 1 1/4 vegetable, 1/4 fruit, 3 fat

Yield: 8 servings

Croutons:
- 1/3 cup (75 mL) dry unseasoned bread crumbs
- 1/3 cup (75 mL) ground walnuts
- 3 logs (3.5 oz./100 g each) goat cheese, cut into 1/2" (1.3 cm) slices
- 3 tablespoons (50 mL) olive oil

- 12 cups (3 L) torn mixed salad greens
- 1/2 cup (125 mL) vinaigrette dressing
- Fresh red raspberries or pomegranate seeds
- Freshly cracked pepper

Hearty Hazelnut Wild Rice

Yield: 10 cups (2.5 L)

- 1 cup (250 mL) golden raisins
- 1/2 cup (125 mL) dry sherry
- 4 1/2 cups (1.125 L) chicken broth
- 1 cup (250 mL) uncooked wild rice, rinsed and drained
- 1 cup (250 mL) uncooked brown rice
- 3 tablespoons (50 mL) butter, divided
- 1 cup (250 mL) coarsely chopped hazelnuts*
- 1/2 cup (125 mL) chopped fresh parsley
- 1/2 teaspoon (2 mL) salt
- 1/4 teaspoon (1 mL) pepper

In a small saucepan, bring raisins and sherry to a boil over medium heat. Simmer for 5 minutes. Cover. Remove from heat. Set aside.

In 4-quart (4 L) saucepan, combine broth, rices, and 2 tablespoons (25 mL) butter. Bring to a boil over high heat. Cover. Reduce heat to medium-low. Simmer for 35 to 45 minutes, or until rice is tender and broth is absorbed.

Meanwhile, melt remaining tablespoon (15 mL) butter in skillet over medium heat. Add nuts and sauté for 4 to 5 minutes, or until toasted. Add raisins with sherry, toasted nuts, parsley, salt, and pepper to cooked rice just before serving.

You may substitute another nut, such as almonds or pecans, for hazelnuts.

Per 1/2 Cup (125 mL): Calories: 151 • Protein: 3 g. • Carbohydrate: 20 g. • Fat: 6 g.
• Cholesterol: 5 mg. • Sodium: 304 mg.
Exchanges: 1 starch, 1/3 fruit, 1 1/4 fat

Double Berry Mousse

Yield: 10 servings

- 1 envelope unflavored gelatin
- 2 tablespoons (25 mL) cold water
- 1/4 cup (60 mL) fresh lemon juice
- 2 cups (500 mL) frozen strawberries, thawed
- 2 cups (500 mL) frozen raspberries, thawed
- 2 tablespoons (25 mL) orange liqueur or orange juice concentrate
- 2 teaspoons (10 mL) grated lemon peel
- 3 egg yolks
- 1/2 cup (125 mL) sugar
- 2 cups (500 mL) heavy cream
- Strawberry fans*

In medium saucepan, combine gelatin and water. Let stand 5 minutes. Whisk in lemon juice. Stir in berries, liqueur, and lemon peel. Bring to a simmer over medium-high heat, stirring often. Let cool to room temperature.

Combine yolks and sugar in small mixing bowl. Beat at medium speed of electric mixer for 3 to 5 minutes, or until pale yellow. Place mixture in the top of a double boiler or in a saucepan set over a second saucepan filled with 2" (5 cm) of simmering water. Cook for 8 to 10 minutes, or until hot and slightly thickened, whisking constantly. Set aside to cool.

Whip cream until soft peaks form. Gently stir berry mixture into egg mixture. Combine them, but don't overmix. Stir a large scoop of whipped cream into berry-egg mixture. Fold remaining whipped cream into mixture. Spoon mousse into ramekins or wine glasses. Cover with plastic wrap. Chill for several hours until set. Garnish with strawberry fans.

To make strawberry fans, clean whole strawberries, leaving stems attached. Cut narrow slices lengthwise into strawberries, leaving berries intact at stem end. Press gently on berries to fan them.

Per Serving: Calories: 257 • Protein: 3 g. • Carbohydrate: 19 g. • Fat: 19 g. • Cholesterol: 129 mg. • Sodium: 22 mg.
Exchanges: 3/4 fruit, 4 fat, 1/2 other carbohydrate

Entertaining Help

Table Setting

Making and Folding Napkins

Fresh Flower Basics

Ribbons and Bows

Schedules and Checklists

Holiday Beverages

Table Setting

The universal "rules" for the arrangement of plates, flatware, and glassware at each place setting are designed for convenience and efficiency, at least for right-handed people. Because the settings are followed consistently, left-handed people become accustomed to the placement and adapt their eating mannerisms. A change in the expected arrangement would cause confusion and reflect unfavorably on the entertaining savvy of the host. Napkin folding and placement (page 134), however, offer a chance for creativity.

Use only the tableware items necessary for the menu, including a glass for each beverage you intend to serve. Some items, such as the dessert plate and fork and coffee cups and saucers, may be brought to each setting after the main plates are cleared. Arrange flatware in the order in which each piece will be used, progressing from the outside in toward the plate.

Informal Place Setting

In anticipation of a relaxed serving style and simple meal, an informal place setting includes these elements. The dinner plate is in the center of the setting, about 2" (5 cm) from the table edge or centered on a placemat. Flatware is arranged in order of use, from outside inward, with handles aligned to the plate edge. Forks are to the left of the plate; the salad fork on the far left indicates the meal will be started with a salad. The knife, with cutting edge inward, is placed to the right of the plate. If a spoon is needed for the meal, it is placed to the right of the knife. The napkin, with folded edge inward, rests to the left of the forks. A beverage glass is slightly above and to the left of the knife tip.

Optional Settings

You may opt to set each place with a charger, setting the plate or bowl for each course on the charger as the meal progresses.

Alternatively, salad or soup may be served before seating, with the plate or bowl set in the center of the dinner plate or charger.

Formal Place Setting

A formal setting indicates a more sophisticated serving style and a more complex meal. The soup spoon to the right of the knife indicates soup will be served. A bread plate and knife are placed above the forks. Wine glasses in front of the water glass indicate that white wine will be served with the first course, followed by red wine. A dessert spoon and/or fork are placed above the plate, parallel to the table edge; the fork handle to the left, the spoon handle to the right.

Glassware

Stemmed glassware designed for a specific purpose is distinguished by its shape. From left to right: oversized balloon glass for water; rounded glass for burgundy wine; straight-sided glass for white wine; all-purpose wineglass; Champagne flute; snifter (for brandy or Cognac); dessert wine glass.

Making and Folding Napkins

While paper napkins are perfectly suitable for informal gatherings, occasions seem more special when you use cloth napkins. Purchasing cloth dinner napkins at perhaps $4.00 each for a party of twelve people can take a chunk out of your party budget. However, you can make all twelve napkins for around $10.00, with fabric of your choice and one free evening.

Dinner napkins range in size from 16" to 20" (40.5 to 51 cm); cocktail napkins are about 12" (30.5 cm). Look for fabric that measures at least 48" (122 cm) across so you can cut three dinner napkins or four cocktail napkins from one width of fabric. Though cloth napkins are often reversible, printed fabrics are also suitable. Natural fiber fabric, such as cotton or linen, is absorbent and easily laundered.

Serger Method

1. Mark napkin dimensions on the fabric, following the grainlines. Use pencil or chalk on tightly woven fabric; pull threads on loosely woven fabric. Leave a small margin on the fabric ends.

2. Set serger for a balanced 3-thread overlock, 4 to 5 mm wide and 1 mm long. Thread both loopers with texturized nylon thread; use regular thread in the needle. Test and adjust.

3. Serge on marked lines across the fabric, cutting it into strips; serge the unfinished edges. Then serge each strip into square napkins, leaving tail chains at corners. Serge the unfinished edges of each napkin.

4. Thread tail chains onto a darning needle and draw back under stitches at corners.

Conventional Method

1. Cut napkin 1" (2.5 cm) larger than desired finished size, following grainlines.

2. Press under $\frac{1}{4}$" (6 mm) double-fold hem on each side. Unfold corner; fold diagonally so inner pressed folds align. Press the diagonal fold; trim corner as shown. Repeat at each corner.

3. Refold, mitering corners. Stitch close to inner fold, pivoting at corners.

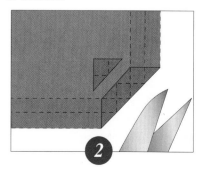

Butterfly Fold

1. With the napkin right side up, accordion-pleat diagonally from corner to corner.

2. Fold in half, and insert into napkin ring, allowing sides to flair out gracefully.

Bishop's Hat and Fleur-de-lis Fold

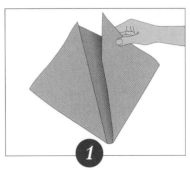

3. Curve sides to back and tuck one inside the other, forming circular base; stand upright. This completes a Bishop's Hat Fold.

4. Fold down the two front points, to form the Fleur-de-lis Fold.

1. Fold in half diagonally, right side out, with fold at bottom. Bring bottom points to meet top point.

2. Fold up lower point to 1" (2.5 cm) below top point. Fold lower point back to meet bottom fold.

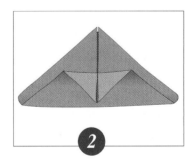

Tiered Points Fold

1. Fold napkin in half, right side out; fold in half again. Turn on the diagonal, so all open corners are at bottom.

2. Fold back first layer, aligning point to the top corner. Fold back each layer in turn, so all points are spaced 1" (2.5 cm) apart.

3. Fold sides under.

Fresh Flower Basics

Fresh flowers add a luxurious touch to your holiday party. Using year-round and seasonal varieties purchased from the florist, you can create beautiful arrangements to decorate the dining room table, coffee table, or buffet.

A centerpiece on the dining room table is usually short so it does not interfere with conversation, and because it is seen from all sides, it is usually symmetrical. A buffet arrangement can be taller for more impact. It, too, should be symmetrical if the buffet is in the center of the room. If the buffet table is against a wall, the arrangement can be three-sided.

The long-lasting flowers listed at right are excellent choices because they can be arranged ahead of time. If the arrangement will be made in advance, select compact blossoms that will open to full beauty by the day of your party. Sprigs of greenery, such as Scotch pine, spruce, or juniper are appropriate additions for holiday arrangements. Canella berries, decorative pods, pepper berries, pinecones, feathers, and seeded eucalyptus offer festive embellishment.

Fresh Flower Tips

• Cut rose stems diagonally under water, at least 2" (5 cm) from the end, using a sharp knife. When stems are not cut under water, air bubbles form at the ends, preventing water from rising up the stems.

• Cut stems for most fresh flowers diagonally, using a sharp knife, to increase water absorption. Snap the stems of chrysanthemums.

• Remove any stems that will be covered by water or floral foam; leaves left in the water will shorten the life of the flowers.

• Remove stamens from lilies to prevent pollen from falling on and discoloring petals and table linens.

• Crush the stem ends of woody plants and evergreens with a hammer to increase water absorption.

• Add cut-flower food to the water, and add fresh water daily. Keep arrangements out of direct sunlight. With the exception of orchids and succulents, mist the blossoms in the arrangement to keep them fresh longer.

Long-Lasting Fresh Flowers		
Variety	**Available Colors**	**Lasts**
Alstroemeria	Many colors	8 to 10 days
Baby's Breath	White	7 to 14 days
Carnation	Many colors	7 to 14 days
Chrysanthemum	Many colors	10 to 12 days
Freesia	Yellow, Pink, Purple, and White	5 to 7 days
Heather	Purple and Mauve	10 to 14 days
Leptosporum	White and Reddish Pink	5 to 7 days
Lily	Many colors	7 to 10 days
Orchids	Many colors	5 to 10 days
Ornithogalum	White, Yellow, and Pink	10 to 14 days
Rose	Many colors	5 to 7 days
Star-of-Bethlehem	White	10 to 14 days
Statice	Many colors	14 to 21 days
Yarrow	White and Yellow	10 to 14 days

Fresh Flower Arrangements

What You'll Need

- Flowers in three sizes
- Sprigs of two or more varieties of greenery
- Gilded pods, berries, or twigs, for short arrangement
- Tall linear floral material, such as gilded devil's claw heliconia, curly willow, or branches, for tall arrangement
- Floral foam designed for fresh flowers, for short arrangement
- Wide-mouth vase for tall arrangement
- Floral tape
- Sharp knife

Short Arrangement

1. Soak floral foam in water containing flower food for thirty minutes. Cut foam, using knife, so it fits container and extends 1" (2.5 cm) above rim. Secure with floral tape.

2. Cut greenery sprigs 5" to 8" (12.5 to 20.5 cm); trim away any stems near ends. Insert sprigs into foam, with longer sprigs around outside and shorter sprigs near center.

3. Insert largest flowers into foam, placing one stem in center and several stems on each side to establish height and width of arrangement. Space remaining large flowers evenly.

4. Insert smaller flowers into arrangement, one variety at a time, spacing evenly, so arrangement appears balanced from all sides.

5. Fill bare areas with greenery. Accent with pods, twigs, or berries.

Tall Arrangement

1. Make a grid over mouth of vase, using floral tape, to support and separate stems. Insert greenery into vase, with taller stems at center back and shorter stems at sides and front. Add linear material, spacing evenly.

2. Space flowers evenly throughout, inserting largest variety first. Keep arrangement balanced on three sides. Fill bare areas with smallest flowers.

Ribbons and Bows

Ribbon adds flair and character to your crafting and decorating projects. A simple wreath, garland, or swag goes from ordinary to extraordinary with the addition of a colorful ribbon tied up in an abundant bow with flowing tails. Ribbon bows can also be used as splashy accents on candlesticks, stemware, or even chair backs.

Craft ribbon is available in several fabric types, including taffeta, moiré, satin, and velvet. For a country look, bows can be made from paper twist. Some weatherproof ribbons are suitable for outdoor projects. Wired ribbon, also called French ribbon, has fine wires running along both edges that enable it to retain twists, loops, and folds as you style it. This feature, you will find, is worth the added expense.

Traditional Bow

1. Cut 18" (46 cm) length of ribbon; set aside for the center tie. Fold a 4" (10 cm) loop in the end of the remaining ribbon, right side out, leaving an 8" (20.5 cm) tail. Fold a second loop toward the opposite side, bringing the ribbon underneath the tail to keep the right side of the ribbon facing out.

2. Continue wrapping ribbon, making loops that fan slightly, until there are three or four loops on each side with a second tail extending. Twist wire tightly around the center, gathering the ribbon in.

3. At the center of the 18" (46 cm) ribbon piece, fold in the sides and wrap the piece around the center of the bow, knotting it in the back.

4. Separate the loops and trim the tails as desired.

If you think you can't tie the perfect bow, think again. Here are some easy step-by-step directions to help you tie two festive styles: a traditional bow and a cluster bow. The key to achieving a luxurious look is to be generous with the ribbon. The size of the bow should be in proportion to the project. A traditional bow that spans 7" to 8" (18 to 20.5 cm) requires 2½ to 3 yd. (2.3 to 2.75 m) of ribbon, 2" to 2½" (5 to

6.5 cm) wide. To determine the ribbon required for a cluster bow, multiply the desired diameter times the number of loops desired. Add 6" (15 cm) to this measurement for the center loop plus the desired amount for tails and any extra streamers. You will also need floral wire or chenille wire to hold the bows together.

Cluster Bow

1. Make a 5" (12.5 cm) loop, leaving a long tail. Pinch the ribbon together at the base of the loop and twist a 12" (30.5 cm) length of wire, centered, around it; spread the wire tails apart.

2. Make a second loop; pinch the base, wrap a wire tail around it, and twist the wire tails together once. If your ribbon is not reversible,

twist it so the right side is always out before you form each loop.

3. Continue making loops, securing each with the wire, until your bow reaches the desired size. As you wrap each loop, alternate the wire tails, so they remain fairly even in length. Cut the ribbon, leaving another long tail.

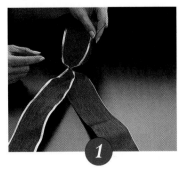

Schedules and Checklists

Some of us are born list makers, going so far as to write down reminders to make lists. Others of us boast the ability to "keep it all in our heads." No matter where you fall in the scale, commit to writing out task schedules and shopping lists when you plan a party, if for no other reason than to preserve your sanity. Checking off items on a to-do list can be rewarding in itself, but pulling off a successful party without a single hitch is an accomplishment to brag about. It's also a well-kept secret that the process of orchestrating the perfect party is often more entertaining than the party itself, but your guests don't need to know that!

The following timetable is a good place to get you started. You may have other tasks to include, relative to the size and theme of the party or other special circumstances. Aside from this checklist, create separate detailed shopping lists for menu items, bar items, decorating items and crafting materials. Most likely you will be shopping in different locations for the items on each list.

Helping Hands

Making it all come together smoothly is an insurmountable task for one person, but "doable" for two. One host cannot be two places at once, for instance taking care of last minute food preparation while greeting guests at the door. It's equally as hard to mix drinks at the bar while stoking the fire. Yet you want your guests to feel catered to from the minute they enter. So enlist the help of your significant other, one or two close friends who also happen to be guests, or a couple of responsible teenagers. There is nothing worse than missing your own party!

Party Planning Timetable

3 Weeks Before:

❑ Determine the party theme.

❑ Plan the menu.

❑ Look for decorating ideas; plan handcrafted items.

❑ Create a guest list and mail invitations.

❑ Decide what you will wear.

2 Weeks Before:

❑ Select recipes and make a grocery list.

❑ Make a shopping list and shop for decorations and craft materials (other than fresh plant materials).

❑ Make any handcrafted items, such as favors, ornaments, artificial wreaths, place cards, or table linens.

1 Week Before:

❑ Finalize the guest list.

❑ Buy non-perishable groceries and bar items.

❑ Prepare and freeze/store any menu items that can be made in advance.

❑ Select and inspect all tableware and serving pieces.

❑ Plan the seating arrangement or buffet table layout.

❑ Order fresh flowers.

2 Days Before:

❑ Clean out the refrigerator.

❑ Buy any fresh fruit that needs to ripen.

❑ Pick up flowers and other fresh plant material needed for decorations.

❑ Make centerpieces, wreaths, or other fresh floral accents.

1 Day Before:

❑ Clean and decorate the house.

❑ Press table linens; fold napkins.

❑ Set the dining table or set out serving pieces on the buffet table.

❑ Thaw frozen menu items.

❑ Buy any fresh baked goods.

❑ Make room in the coat closet.

Party Day:

❑ Prepare the food following a detailed time schedule.

❑ Set up the bar; chill beverages as necessary.

❑ Run and empty the dishwasher.

❑ Empty garbage cans.

❑ Bring in firewood.

❑ Stock bathrooms with guest towels, soap, and extra toilet paper.

❑ Select music.

Holiday Beverages

Hot Buttered Rum

Yield: 20 to 22 servings

- 2 cups (500 mL) vanilla ice cream
- 1 cup (250 mL) (2 sticks) butter, softened
- 1 1/4 cups (300 mL) packed brown sugar
- 2 cups (500 mL) powdered sugar
- 1 teaspoon (5 mL) ground nutmeg
- 1 teaspoon (5 mL) ground cinnamon
- 1/2 teaspoon (2 mL) ground cloves
- 1 1/4 cups (300 mL) or more dark rum
- Boiling water
- Cinnamon sticks

Let ice cream soften slightly. In large bowl, cream butter and brown sugar together. Beat in powdered sugar, nutmeg, cinnamon, and cloves. Stir in ice cream until smooth. Place batter in plastic container and freeze until ready to use. (Mixture will remain spoonable.)

To serve, spoon 3 tablespoons (50 mL) batter into mug. Add 1 tablespoon (15 mL) rum (or more to taste). Fill mug with boiling water (about ¾ cup/175 mL). Add cinnamon stick to mug to use as a stirrer.

Variation: For a non-alcoholic version, place 2 or 3 tablespoons (25 or 50 mL) batter in mug and top with hot apple cider. Stir to combine.

Holiday Mimosas

Yield: 18 servings

- 4 cups (1 L) cranberry juice
- 2 cups (500 mL) freshly squeezed orange juice, strained
- 2 bottles (750 mL each) champagne or sparkling wine, chilled

Combine juices in a pitcher. Chill. To serve, fill champagne flutes half full with champagne (⅓ cup/75 mL). Top with juice mixture (about ⅓ cup/75 mL).

Tom and Jerrys

Yield: 20 servings

- 6 very fresh eggs
- ⅔ cup (150 mL) powdered sugar, divided
- 1 1/2 cups (375 mL) brandy, divided
- 15 cups (3.75 L) milk or water
- Ground nutmeg

Separate egg yolks and whites into separate large bowls. Beat whites at medium speed of electric mixer until frothy. Gradually beat in ⅓ cup (75 mL) sugar. Beat at high speed until whites form stiff peaks. Set aside.

Clean beaters. Beat yolks with remaining ⅓ cup (75 mL) sugar and ¼ cup (60 mL) brandy until light and lemon-colored. Stir a scoop of whites into yolks with a whisk to lighten the yolks. Fold remaining whites into yolks.

In large pot, heat milk over medium heat just until steaming, stirring occasionally. (Do not boil.) Reduce heat to low.

To serve, spoon 1 tablespoon (15 mL) brandy (or more to taste) and ¼ cup (60 mL) egg mixture into mug. Stir in ¾ cup (175 mL) hot milk. Sprinkle top with nutmeg.

Notes: This traditional beverage is for brandy lovers. Rum or whiskey can also be substituted for brandy.

If using raw eggs concerns you, use pasteurized eggs. Egg substitutes will not work.

Tangy Cranberry Punch

Yield: 12 cups (3 L)

- 3 cups (750 mL) fresh or frozen cranberries
- 3 cups (750 mL) water
- $1\frac{1}{2}$ cups (375 mL) sugar
- 6 cups (1.5 L) ginger ale, chilled
- 1 cup (250 mL) sour carbonated beverage, chilled

In a 4-quart (4 L) saucepan, combine cranberries, water, and sugar. Bring to a simmer over medium heat, stirring until sugar is dissolved. Simmer, partially covered, over medium heat for 8 to 10 minutes, or until cranberries are popped and pulpy. Stir and press cranberries occasionally. Strain mixture through fine-mesh strainer. Discard pulp. Chill juice.

Just before serving, combine cranberry juice in punch bowl with ginger ale and sour.

Note: This is a very tangy punch. For a little less tartness, omit sour and add just ginger ale to cranberry juice.

Tip: To keep punch cold, make an ice ring by freezing fruit (cherries, Mandarin oranges, lemon slices, pineapple chunks) in a ring mold filled with water or cranberry juice cocktail. Or make small fruited ices by freezing fruit and liquid in custard cups or a muffin tin.

Hot Spiced Cider

Yield: 8 cups (2 L)

Sachet:
- 2 sticks cinnamon, broken
- 2 teaspoons (10 mL) whole cloves
- 1 teaspoon (5 mL) whole allspice
- Peel of 1 lemon

- 2 medium red apples
- 1 orange
- 1 bottle (64 oz./1.892 L) apple cider
- $\frac{1}{3}$ cup (75 mL) pure maple syrup
- Cinnamon sticks (optional)

Place sachet ingredients on a piece of cheesecloth or in a paper coffee filter. Bundle and tie sachet closed with long piece of kitchen twine. Core apples and cut crosswise into $\frac{1}{2}$" (1.3 cm) slices. Cut slices in half. Thinly slice orange. Cut slices in half. Set aside.

In large pot, combine apple cider, maple syrup, and apple slices. Add sachet, tying end of string to handle of pot. Bring to a boil over high heat. Reduce heat to medium–low. Simmer for 10 to 12 minutes, or just until apples are tender.

Remove sachet before serving. Ladle hot cider into mugs. Add an apple and orange slice to each mug. If desired, add a cinnamon stick to each mug.

Cinnamon Coffee Float

Yield: 1 serving

- $\frac{1}{2}$ cup (125 mL) vanilla ice cream
- $\frac{1}{8}$ teaspoon (0.5 mL) ground cinnamon
- $\frac{3}{4}$ cup (175 mL) hot brewed coffee
- Cinnamon stick

Place ice cream and ground cinnamon in a mug. Pour hot coffee over top. Add cinnamon stick to use as a stirrer.

Variations: Substitute cinnamon ice cream for vanilla ice cream and ground cinnamon. It is often available seasonally.

Chocolate ice cream is also a good substitute for vanilla.

Index